Understanding the Financial Life Cycle of Your Business

By

Ariel Antonio Planz de Bethencourt

© 2021 by Ariel Antonio Planz

All rights reserved. Neither this book nor any portion thereof may be reproduced or used in any manner whatsoever without the prior express written permission of the author.

Library of Congress Registration Number TXu 2-340-486

 Zephir Press

PO Box 37459
Oak Park, CA 91377

Foreword	Page 1
Introduction	Page 5
The Income Statement	Page 11
The Balance Sheet	Page 21
The Breakeven Point	Page 31
Product Pricing	Page 49
The Cost-Benefit Analysis	Page 73
The Financial Life Cycle of Your Business	Page 77
The Seed Stage	Page 77
The Outside Financing Stage	Page 82
The Public Offering or Venture Capital Stage	Page 85
Appendix A	Page 94

FOREWORD

One fine summer day, I was talking to one of my clients, who is also a friend, and who owns a small construction company.

I was trying to help him understand what he needed to do in order to be more profitable as well as to be able to get the sort of bank financing that would help his business grow. Invariably, the conversation turned technical. At that moment I noticed that when I started to say financial words his eyes sort of – glazed over, and then he just quietly nodded in an indifferent manner. By that I could tell that all he really wanted, was for this conversation to end and for me to go away.

Obviously, I was not getting through to him.

"What did I just say?" I asked him.

"I don't know. What did you just say?"

Frustrated, "I replied, how are you going to make your business successful if you can't do this stuff?"

"I don't want to do this stuff! He replied, "I want YOU to do this stuff!"

"I charge $150 an hour."

"An hour?" he gasped; jaw falling open and eyes bugging out.

"You bet."

"But I am your friend."

"That price includes my best friend discount."

"Oh!"

"Uh huh." I replied.

After a few moments of thoughtful silence, he finally said, "Then, can you just write it all down for me and use big letters but small words?"

What a brilliant idea! I thought to myself. Hence this book came into being.

There are thousands of businessmen and women who are like my friend and who have their own businesses. Who are daily, struggling to understand what their bookkeepers or accountants are telling them. But also, some of the ideas expressed in the following pages are more sophisticated than what a bookkeeper with and associate in business degree from the local community college would understand. Yet they are very, very important concepts for any businessperson to understand. This book is targeted for the small business owner. The medium to large business owners, (those with revenues between $5,000,000 to $100,000,000 and up) have access to more sophisticated accounting and finance professionals.

Even so, managers of larger businesses – even publicly traded companies, need to understand some of the concepts in this book.

I say this because there was a time in my life when I traveled the United States teaching financial analysis to middle and senior managers of some of the largest companies in the world.

Without fail, when I was conducting one of my courses, there would always be one person who would raise his hand to ask the question, "Is there anything that I can do to avoid having to do all this complicated stuff?"

"You mean like a silver bullet? The silver bullet of financial analysis?"

"Yes, that is it exactly!" He, she, or they would enthusiastically exclaim.

"There is no silver bullet to financial analysis," I would reply, "The big Wall Street banks wouldn't pay Harvard MBAs' a million dollars a year to do this stuff if there was a silver bullet.

That would deflate their balloon. And for sure, when the class came back from the lunch break that person or persons would be missing.

In a sense, however, this was not entirely true. To me, there is a silver bullet and that is what is called, Break Even Analysis, which will be covered in this book.

In my defense however, I will say that Break Even Analysis was included in the subject matter of the courses that I was teaching. Also, the companies that paid me to teach this course to their employees wanted me to teach them a robust curriculum including, Trend Analysis, Cash Flow Analysis, and Ratio Analysis as well as Break Even Analysis. I needed to give full value for the amount of money they paid to have me there for two days as well as for their paying my traveling expenses. So, in my way of thinking, the, "Silver Bullet", was there for them to find – if they had stuck around to the end of the class. If they missed that silver bullet because they left early then that was a bad call on their part.

Now accounting may not be everyone's cup of tea. But accounting is the language of business. That's it. Nothing more. If you are going to live in Spain you better learn the language. If you are going to run your own business, then you also better learn some of the language. Because at the end of the day, and when all is said and done it comes down to dollars and cents. And accounting is how the dollars and cents are measured according to a set of rules. Ultimately, this will measure your success or failure.

I have tried to make the language in this book as simple as possible. The concepts are rudimentary but essential. You don't need to get a degree in accounting or finance in order to understand this book.

But if you do understand the concepts of what is in here then you will have a huge advantage over your competition.

Thank you.

INTRODUCTION

So, you have established a new business. Or ... you are planning to.

Congratulations! You will now experience the most satisfying as well as the most frustrating period of your life.

But, as the old saying goes – nothing which is worthwhile is easy.

Yes, it will not be easy, but it will be satisfying to watch your business grow and succeed if, and this is a big IF, you can avoid the traps and pitfalls of the financial riddle.

There is an old saying; It takes money to make money. Right?

No - not right.

It takes CASH to make money.

So, as we go through this course I would like to you remember two things:

Cash is king.

And

In life you get what you pay for.

So, let's jump right in.

Whatever you are making or whatever service you are providing you will have to organize your business into one of three business categories:

1. <u>Sole Proprietor</u>

    a. Advantages: Pays taxes at the individual rate. Reports profit and loss on IRS Schedule C.
    b. Disadvantages: Unlimited personal liability.

2. <u>Partnership</u>

    a. Advantages: Pays taxes at the individual rate. The partnership gives each partner a Schedule K-1 which he adds to his/her individual tax return.
    b. Disadvantages: Unlimited liability unless he/she is a Limited Partner.

3. <u>Corporation</u>

    a. Advantages: Limited Liability.
    b. Disadvantages: Double taxation because you are taxed at the corporate level as well as at the personal level.

All other forms of business organizations are derivatives of the last two. Whether we are talking about Limited Partnerships, C-Corporations, Subchapter-S Corporations, LLC's, etc.

The legal nuances of what the three different methods of organizing a company are not for this book. Simply let it be said that the easiest and least expensive way to organize a business is Sole Proprietor.

Most start-up businesses do in fact, start up as Sole Proprietors then they morph into something else.

Here is a true-life example (from a lady I used to know):

A lady who is a stay-at-home mom decides that she has a lot of time on her hands and decides to make special apple turnovers the way that her mother taught her a long time ago when she was growing up in Germany.

She starts by making them in her kitchen at home then starts selling them at church functions. They become popular after which she starts to sell them to her neighbors.

All this time she is producing them in her kitchen.

Since this is a home business that was accidentally created, she reports her revenue as well as expenses on her personal tax returns. Specifically, on the IRS Schedule C.

But, in time and as her apple turnovers become more popular she decides to hire some starving students to work for her on a part-time basis to help her meet the increased demand.

Eventually, she decides to rent a commercial space so that she can have an industrial type of kitchen as well as a counter to serve walk-in customers.

One day, one of her customers asks her if he can buy some coffee. She does not serve any. But thinks that it would be a good idea to offer some to her customers. She then decides to buy various coffee machines. Then she also starts to sell juices, soft drinks, etc.

In time, her product line grows to include muffins, freshly baked rolls, and other pastries.

A little while after that she decides to buy some tables and chairs so that her customers can sit down and enjoy the warm apple turnovers and coffee at her location if they want to.

In time her little company grows to four locations throughout the city. But now she also offers freshly made cakes and pies. Custom ordered if her customer wants that. Her target market with the cakes are birthdays and weddings.

And eventually, she also decides to incorporate. When she incorporates she decides to name her company, "Mom's Bakery, Inc.", (Okay, not original but please remember that this is just a book on accounting, and I am not Emily Bronte, and neither is this book Wuthering Heights.)

But here is the problem: Growth requires money. Cash specifically. Where does she get the cash to fund that growth?

Product Sales? She sells her turnovers for about $1.50 each. Yet, to produce each and every one of them she needs to:

1. Buy supplies (raw materials inventory).
2. Pay her employees.
3. Pay the rent – Needs to get paid in advance.
4. Pay the utilities.
5. Buy or rent equipment.
6. Pay other miscellaneous expenses.

So now the big question is: How many of those apple turnovers which sell for $1.50 each does she need to sell to meet all the above listed (as well as other) expenses?

For the purposes of simplification, let's forget her product mix for the moment. In other words, let's forget the coffee, pastries, cakes as well as all the other products she sells. Let's just use the apple turnovers as an example.

You will now be introduced to the most fundamental as well as the most important concept in cost accounting and that is what is called, The Breakeven Point. It is not only a fundamental concept but also a very important concept. Unfortunately, it is not commonly used. Not even by accounting and finance professionals.

The Breakeven Point is defined as: That point in your profit and loss where all your income is the same as all of your expenses so that your net profit is zero. This means that the very next sale that you make 100% of that will be all profit (all of your expenses are already covered).

But before we go any further let's try to understand some basic financial terminology:

There are two basic financial reports that we have to deal with, and they are:

- The Income Statement
- The Balance Sheet

THE INCOME STATEMENT

THE INCOME STATEMENT: The income statement is a report that tells you (and others) what has occurred financially to your company over a certain period of time. That period of time can be one day, or one month, one quarter, or one year.

The basic components of the income statement are (in the following order):

a. Revenue: This is all the sales that your company has experienced over a period of time.

b. Cost of Goods Sold: Here are the expenses necessary to produce the goods that you have sold over that period of time. Or, what it costs to get your products ready to sell.

c. Gross Revenue: All of your Revenue minus the Cost of Sales above.

d. General and Administrative Expenses: All of the expenses that were incurred over that period of time that are not directly related to creating a product or service. Here are the expenses that involve selling the product.

e. Net Profit: Anything left over.

The way that the INCOME STATEMENT is designed is fairly straightforward. It goes from top to bottom.

First, and logically: there are your sales. Also called REVENUE. This section lists what you sold and how much you sold them for.

Below that is a section called COST OF GOODS SOLD. This section lists what items you sold and how much you had to pay TO GET IT READY TO BE SOLD. This section is very important, and we will dive deeper into it in a little while.

The COST OF GOODS SOLD is an expense so we will have to take the REVENUE for the period and then subtract the COST OF GOODS SOLD for the period to get to the next section of the INCOME STATEMENT, which is called GROSS PROFIT.

In summary then: REVENUE – COST OF GOODS SOLD = GROSS PROFIT.

Now comes the good stuff. Because under GROSS PROFIT comes all your other expenses for the period. By other expenses I mean those expenses NOT DIRECTLY CONNECTED TO GETTING YOUR PRODUCT READY TO SELL. In Cost of Goods Sold are only the expenses DIRECTLY CONNECTED in getting your product made, manufactured or ready to sell.

In essence, the income statement is a sifting process. It starts with all of your sales (or revenue), then reduces that by what it costs you to make your products (sifting out some of the revenue). Then it goes on to sift what revenue is left over by all of the other expenses necessary to run your business.

Once the sifting process is over you are left with Net Profit or Net Loss.

Back to our income statement: The section under Gross Profit is normally called GENERAL, SALES & ADMINSTRATIVE EXPENSES. What is in this section includes:

- SALARIES, (managers, salespeople, delivery people, consultants, etc.)
- RENT
- TAXES
- UTILITIES
- AND WHATEVER ELSE WAS NOT INCLUDED IN COST OF GOODS SOLD.

At the very bottom is your NET PROFIT. And this is simply whatever is left over.

In summary then:

REVENUE – COST OF GOODS SOLD = GROSS PROFIT

Then,

GROSS PROFIT – GENERAL, SALES & ADMINISTRATIVE EXPENSES = NET PROFIT

HERE IS A SAMPLE INCOME STATEMENT:

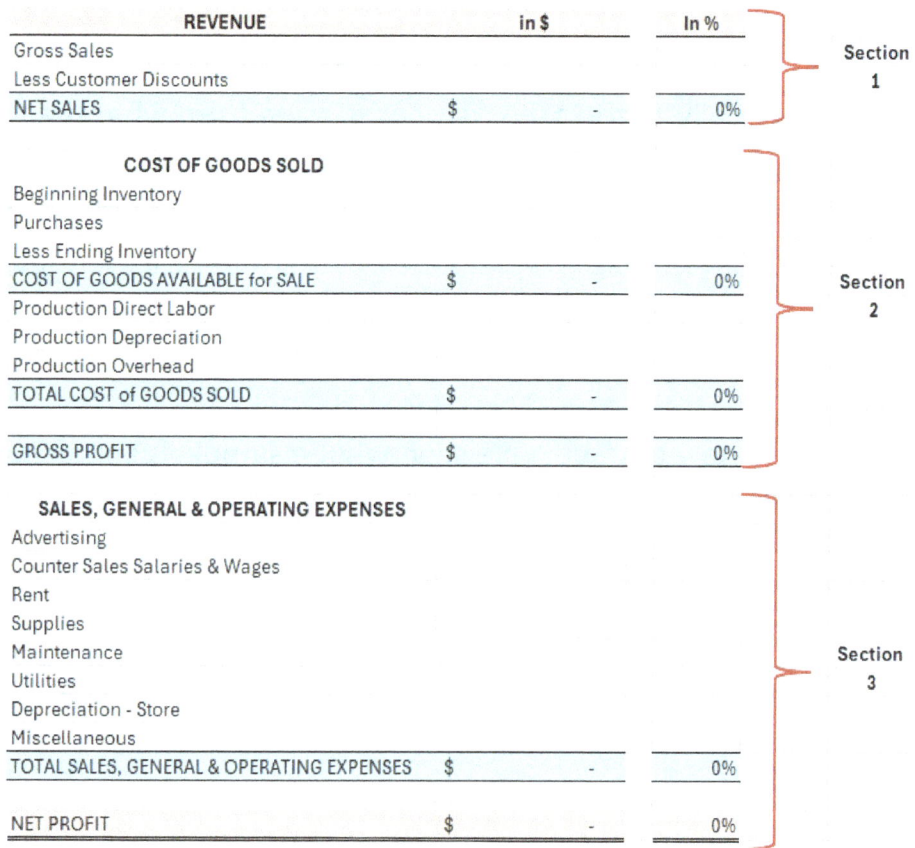

Once again, and as you can see the income statement is divided into three sections. The first section is called, Revenue. This is all of the money brought into the business for a given period without taking into account any expenses.

Section 2, which is the next section down, is where the expenses begin to be taken into account. This section is called, Cost of Goods Sold because in this section are only the expenses that are incurred in directly making what you are selling. This is basically, the raw materials and labor used to transform those raw materials into your finished goods. Ready to be presented to the consumer who will hopefully buy a lot of them. Gross Profit is Revenue less Cost of Goods Sold.

Section 3, is called; Sales, General & Operating Expenses. And this is basically all the other expenses aside from what is already included in Cost of Goods Sold (or COGS for short). At the bottom of Section 3 is the holy grail of capitalism which is Net Profit. (Did you make money or lose money? Can we now lease the Bentley, or will we have to take the bus?)

But now that we have seen what a sample Income Statement looks like let's create one for Mom's Bakery.

Let us say that she has been open for one year and at one location. Each day she sells 100 apple turnovers at $1.50 each. She is open every day of the year which translates into yearly sales of apple turnovers of $54,750. ($1.50 x 100 x 365).

But she also sells other things such as coffee, juices, pastries as well as cakes and pies. But let's just say that altogether for this year she has grossed $267,010 in Revenue. Note: This number was not entirely pulled out of the air. I am basing this on certain experience from what I know. I know for example that coffee tends to sell at about $2.00 a cup (average price – I know that there are small, medium, and large coffees). And that it tends to sell at about twice the amount of your leading product – in this case the apple turnovers. That means that for every apple turnover that she sells she also sells two cups of coffee. This is then $2.00 x 200 x 365 = $146,000. The beauty of coffee is that it takes a minimum amount of work as well as inventory to get it to the customer. That means that the markup for it is very generous and therefore a very profitable item to sell. (Why do you think that Starbucks shares are currently trading at over $115 a share?)

All the other products that she sells have a similar logic tied to the total $267,025 that this particular store has grossed for the year.

IMPORTANT: In a retail location like this you need to have a variety of products for *incidental sales*. Which means that some people might walk in to just buy a cup of coffee and then decide to also buy an apple turnover. Or vice versa. In some industries which offer multiple products there might be a periodic evaluation of which products to continue to offer for sale and which products to discontinue. This is especially true of heavy manufacturing. But in a retail location like this having a good product mix is very important.

BUT: This rule is not set in stone. Because shelf space is limited at some point a retail company will have to decide which products to discontinue.

Since income is important to the rest of this narrative let's take a closer look at each of its parts.

1. Gross Sales: $267,010 This has been partly explained above. But a breakdown is:
    - Apple Turnovers: about 100 sold a day at $1.50 each times 365 days a year is $54,750
    - Coffee: About 200 cups a day at $2.00 each times 365 a year is $146,000.
    - Custom Cakes: One a month for an average of about $200 each is $2,400.

- Other pastries: About 50 a day at $1.28 each times 365 days is $23,360.
- Juices: About 50 a day at $2.00 each times 365 days is $36,500
- Other incidental income is $4,000.
- <u>Grand Total Sales for the year is $267,010</u>

2. <u>Customer Discounts</u>: Loyal customers are given a card that entitles them to a 5% discount.
3. <u>Beginning Inventory</u>: The amount of inventory on hand on January 1 of this year.
4. <u>Purchases</u>: All of the raw material inventory (flour, eggs, shortening, etc.) bought during the course of the year.
5. <u>Ending Inventory</u>: The amount of inventory left over (not sold) which includes all raw materials and finished goods.
6. <u>Production Labor</u>: She has three cooks at minimum wage. (The starving students.)
7. <u>Production Depreciation</u>: The depreciation on the ovens in the kitchen, mixers, etc.
8. <u>Production overhead</u>: Utilities, (water, electricity, the salary of the chef in the kitchen.)
9. <u>Advertising</u>: Business cards, posters, etc.
10. <u>Counter Sales Salaries & Wages</u>: Five employees at minimum wage.
11. <u>Rent</u>: $1,500 a month.
12. <u>Supplies</u>: Cups, napkins, etc.
13. <u>Maintenance</u>: For the equipment.
14. <u>Utilities</u>: These are just shop utilities.
15. <u>Depreciation – Store & Counter</u>: Tables, Chairs, counters, cash registers, etc.
16. <u>Miscellaneous</u>: Anything else.

NOTES:

a. We subtract ending inventory because we want to get the amount of money spend making our products to be sold – in terms of material. The ending inventory in positive form will be in the balance sheet. (Next chapter.)
b. Some companies (heavy manufacturing for instance). Have an inventory account called Work in Progress (or WIP). This is because it takes a long time to transform raw materials into finished goods for those industries.

Now let's put some numbers into our income statement to see what we end up with.

MOM'S BAKERY INCOME STATEMENT – TWELVE MONTHS ENDED 20XX

REVENUE		in $	In %
Gross Sales	$	267,010	100%
Less Customer Discounts	$	(561)	0%
NET SALES	$	266,449	100%
COST OF GOODS SOLD			
Beginning Inventory	$	3,256	1%
Purchases	$	76,000	28%
Less Ending Inventory	$	(2,358)	-1%
COST OF GOODS AVAILABLE for SALE	$	76,898	29%
Production Direct Labor	$	63,510	24%
Production Depreciation	$	3,000	1%
Production Overhead	$	3,000	1%
TOTAL COST of GOODS SOLD	$	146,408	55%
GROSS PROFIT	$	120,041	45%
SALES, GENERAL & OPERATING EXPENSES			
Advertising	$	356	0%
Counter Sales Salaries & Wages	$	65,850	25%
Rent	$	18,000	7%
Supplies	$	12,575	5%
Maintenance	$	79	0%
Utilities	$	596	0%
Depreciation - Store	$	2,000	1%
Miscellaneous	$	287	0%
TOTAL SALES, GENERAL & OPERATING EXPENSES	$	99,743	37%
NET PROFIT	$	20,298	8%

Not too bad is it? We ended up with a net profit of $20,298. After all is said and done. That is pretty good for a small business which is relatively new. The only thing we have to worry about now is taxes. (Bummer right?)

NOTE:

The Gross Profit on Mom's Bakery is 45%, which is perhaps a little unrealistic. But for what we are going to do it will suffice. Different industries have different levels of Gross Profit. As you will see later – Gross Profit is a VERY important factor in business profitability and survival.

In restaurants for example, the Gross Profit can be anywhere from 3% to 23% of Revenue.

In Manufacturing it can be anywhere from 25% to 55% of Revenue.

In Retail it can be from 3% to 15% of Revenues.

The range in Gross Profit per industry can be very broad because there are different segments within each industry. In Manufacturing for example, there is light manufacturing (low Gross Profit) to heavy manufacturing (high gross profit). In our theoretical company – Mom's Bakery – is a business which is somewhere in a grey area between restaurant, light manufacturing, and retail.

If you wish, you may subscribe to a service offered by a company called, Risk Management Association (or RMA). It used to be called

Robert Morris Associates (after the famous Revolutionary War financier – Robert Morris).

RMA publishes a series of studies on what the average financial statements are for a given industry. These studies (sample financial statements) are presented in percent format not in dollar format. You can take one of these averaged financial statements to see if your company falls within the average for your industry by comparing their percentages to your company's percentages. That is one reason why the percentage numbers to the right of the dollar amounts on our income statement are important. You can find the RMA website on the internet.

THE BALANCE SHEET

<u>THE BALANCE SHEET</u>: The balance sheet is a report that tells you – as well as others - what the financial condition of your company is at a certain period in time.

Which means that the basic difference between the two reports is that the income statement tells you what has happened financially to your company **over a period** of time – say for example – a year or a month or a day. And the balance sheet tells you what your company looks like at the end of that period of time. Or, at the end of that year or month or day (**at a point in time**). To use a metaphor, the income statement is a movie, and the balance sheet is a picture of the end credits.

The basic components of the balance sheet are (in the following order):

a. <u>Assets</u>: These are all of the things your company owns such as cash, furniture, real estate, etc.
b. <u>Liabilities</u>: These are all of the debts that your company has.
c. <u>Equity</u>: This is what is left over. Basically – how much of the company you actually own.

Within the above three categories (Assets, Liabilities and Equity) there are sub-components. Each sub-component is listed in order of greatest liquidity.

For example: within the component named assets there are various types of assets. These are current assets and non-current assets.

The current assets are listed first. (The accounts with the most liquidity go first).

The most liquid asset that exists is cash. Which means that all of your bank accounts (checking and savings) go here. Long-term cash accounts such as certificates of deposit go into non-current assets.

After cash, the most liquid asset is accounts receivable. After accounts receivable comes inventory.

Following the Current Assets section comes Non-Current Assets.

These normally include land, buildings, furniture, equipment, etc.

Following the Asset section comes the Liability section. Again, these are listed in order of liquidity. Or, because they are liabilities – in order of what needs to get paid soonest.

The list is usually headed by Accounts Payable. This is normally followed by Accrued Expenses. After which other long- term liabilities follow such as Mortgages, Long Term Loans, etc.

The Equity section is how much ownership you and everyone else who has invested in your business has. If you have friends or family members who have invested in the business then their percentage of investment would go here.

HERE IS SAMPLE BALANCE SHEET

Your Company Name — **Balance Sheet**

Assets		
Current assets:	Previous Year	Current Year
Cash	-	-
Investments	-	-
Inventories	-	-
Accounts receivable	-	-
Pre-paid expenses	-	-
Other	-	-
Total current assets	-	-
Fixed assets:	Previous Year	Current Year
Property and equipment	-	-
Leasehold improvements	-	-
Equity and other investments	-	-
Less accumulated depreciation	-	-
Total fixed assets	-	-
Other assets:	Previous Year	Current Year
Goodwill	-	-
Total other assets	-	-
Total assets	**-**	**-**

Liabilities and owner's equity		
Current liabilities:	Previous Year	Current Year
Accounts payable	-	-
Accrued wages	-	-
Accrued compensation	-	-
Income taxes payable	-	-
Unearned revenue	-	-
Other	-	-
Total current liabilities	-	-
Long-term liabilities:	Previous Year	Current Year
Mortgage payable	-	-
Total long-term liabilities	-	-
Owner's equity:	Previous Year	Current Year
Investment capital	-	-
Accumulated retained earnings	-	-
Total owner's equity	-	-
Total liabilities and owner's equity	**-**	**-**

And now one filled out for Mom's Bakery.

MOM'S BAKERY — **BALANCE SHEET**

Assets

Current assets:	Previous Year	Current Year
Cash	5,364.00	3,569.00
Inventories	6,358.00	12,235.00
Accounts receivable	-	-
Pre-paid expenses	5,433.00	6,322.00
Other	656.23	788.32
Total current assets	**17,811.23**	**22,914.32**

Fixed assets:	Previous Year	Current Year
Property and equipment	35,699.00	35,699.00
Leasehold improvements	12,322.00	12,322.00
Less accumulated depreciation	2,399.00	3,348.00
Total fixed assets	**50,420.00**	**51,369.00**

Other assets:	Previous Year	Current Year
Goodwill	-	-
Total other assets	-	-
Total assets	**68,231.23**	**74,283.32**

Liabilities & owner's equity

Current liabilities:	Previous Year	Current Year
Accounts payable	3,483.00	7,453.00
Accrued wages	5,988.00	6,433.00
Income taxes payable	2,247.00	1,358.00
Total current liabilities	**11,718.00**	**15,244.00**

Long-term liabilities:	Previous Year	Current Year
Leases payable	2,366.00	1,895.00
Total long-term liabilities	**2,366.00**	**1,895.00**

Owner's equity:	Previous Year	Current Year
Investment capital	41,448.23	41,448.23
Accumulated retained earnings	12,699.00	15,696.09
Total owner's equity	**54,147.23**	**57,144.32**
Total liabilities & owner's equity	**68,231.23**	**74,283.32**

Let us go through each item on the balance sheet so that we can become a little bit more familiar with it.

- <u>Cash</u>: Is exactly that. It is how much cash Mom's Bakery has available in her checking account at the bank.
- <u>Inventories</u>: Mostly raw flour, eggs, milk, shortening, etc. Everything Mom's Bakery needs in order to make her merchandise. The finished goods, (cakes, turnovers, etc.) are consumed on a daily basis. Any left over are usually thrown away after a few days. This goes back to our discussion of quality versus profit. Baked goods taste better if they are freshly baked, and most customers prefer it that way. In this case, Mom's Bakery has decided to give up some profit – that is throw away some unsold baked goods before they get too old – in order to keep her products fresh and to build up her reputation for quality goods. Alternatively, she can sell some of the left-over baked goods from the previous day at half price off. This way people would have a choice and Mom's Bakery does not have to have a complete loss on unsold baked goods.

- <u>Accounts Receivable</u>: This is what her customers owe her. Mom's is a cash and carry operation. Therefore, she would have no receivables.

- <u>Prepaid Expenses</u>: These are expenses that are paid before they are actually due. Why would anyone in their right mind do that? There are various reasons for this. One which comes to mind is property taxes. Mom's Bakery leases her shop. But the lease states that she is responsible for the property taxes. Property taxes are normally due twice a year, in April and then again in November. You can if you wish, pay them for the entire year. In which case, the amounts that are not due yet would go in here.

- Other: Whatever does not fit into any of the above categories.

- Goodwill: This is a category that usually applies to companies that buy other companies. When a company buys another company there is usually a premium that is in excess of the actual value of the company being purchased. Say for example, that company A buys company B. Company B is actually only worth $5,000,000. But company A is willing to pay $7,000,000 for it. The difference of $2,000,000 would go into Goodwill. Yes, basically a plug, (please don't laugh, a plug is a respected and time-honored accounting tool.) Mom's Bakery is a startup therefore there would be no Goodwill here.

- Accounts Payable: This is what Mom's Bakery owes to her vendors. In this case it would be the companies that supply her with her flour, milk, etc. Also, maybe utility bills that have been received and not actually paid yet. Anything where the bill has been received but not paid yet will go here.

- Accrued Wages: Mom's Bakery pays her employees every two weeks, but she keeps track of what she owes her employees on a weekly basis. Also, at the end of the month there is always a cut-off date for preparing the financial statements (Balance Sheet and Income Statement). Whatever that cut-off date is there will always be an amount that we need to estimate as to how much we owe our employees as of that date. For some companies, (i.e. manufacturing for example) this is both an art and a science. That is because certain companies have a lot of overtime as well as temporary labor.

We don't know what the actual amounts are as of that cut-off date because the payroll companies don't calculate the payroll on a daily basis. Therefore, we will need to make an estimate of it. That is called an accrual.

- <u>Income Taxes Payable</u>: When you have employees you have to match (as an employer) the withholding that is mandatory for them. It is mandatory that an employee pay a 6.2% withholding of their gross wages for Social Security and an additional 1.45% for Medicare. The employer has to match these amounts for each and every employee. These are withheld for every payroll (in this case every two weeks) but are usually paid quarterly. Therefore, the amount owed to the government goes here.

- <u>Leases Payable</u>: Mom's Bakery has leased some of the equipment in the kitchen. She has also leased a used delivery truck. The remaining debt on the leases (she pays monthly) goes here. It should be noted that the powers that be in the accounting profession and the ones that dictate the rules for the profession have decided that are now new reporting requirements for operating leases and they are going to be WAY more complicated. The new rules are not for this small book therefore I am not going to get into that. Also, there are differences between capital leases and operating leases. Operating leases are leases such as your rent for the store. Capital leases are very complicated and usually have many financial as well as legal and tax gizmos that go with them. We will not talk about them in this book. (For the sake of the sanity of all involved).

- <u>Investment Capital</u>: This is the amount of money that mom invested in her bakery. This amount will usually never change.

- <u>Accumulated Retained Earnings</u>: When Mom's Bakery makes a profit this is where it goes. If she makes a loss this is where it goes also. Except that the number would be negative. This will change periodically according to how often she closes her accounting records.

Some financial professionals will bet their lives on the Balance Sheet. They will say that if the balance sheet is okay then everything is fine.

I disagree. First of all, the Balance Sheet will be different for every company in every industry. In a manufacturing company for example, we would expect Current Assets to exceed Current Liabilities. As an example, let's say that the Current Assets are as follows:

CURRENT ASSETS	
Cash	$ 500,000
Accounts Receivable	$ 890,650
Inventory	$ 1,023,654
TOTAL CURRENT ASSETS	$ 2,414,304

And that Current Liabilities are as follows:

CURRENT LIABILITIES	
Accounts Payable	$ 256,000
Accruals	$ 385,000
Other	$ 578,365
TOTAL CURRENT LIABILITIES	$ 1,219,365

One of the standard measurements of the health of a company is to see what their WORKING CAPITAL is. Quite simply, Working Capital is the difference between Total Current Assets and Total Current Liabilities. In the example above that would be: $2,414,304 - $1,219,365 = $1,194,939.

Well, to most people that is a very healthy company. I mean if you see that their Current Assets exceeds their Current Liabilities by $1,194,939 then that company is in good financial shape. (Has the means to cover their short-term obligations.)

But what if the company is a restaurant. Restaurants don't have Accounts Receivable or much inventory. That means that their Current Assets probably look like this:

CURRENT ASSETS	
Cash	$ 500,000
Inventory	$ 23,600
TOTAL CURRENT ASSETS	$ 523,600

Which means, that if we leave the Current Liabilities the same as before that their Working Capital would be $523,600-$1,219,365 = -$695,765 (**negative** $695,765)

Their working capital is in the hole! Does that mean that this company will not be successful? And if so, why is McDonalds so successful? Or any of the other large chain restaurants that we know about. Even high-end ones like, The Grill or BJ's Brewhouse?

Obviously, this is open for debate. And the second point that I will make is that even though the Balance Sheet is open for debate the fact is that profit is profit. And a company that is CONSISTENLY profitable will normally be in good shape.

We will leave the Balance Sheet aside for now. We are not going to need it for the discussions that follow.

But it is important to point out that the Balance Sheet and the Income Statement go hand in hand. Money flows from the income statement to the balance sheet and vice versa.

THE BREAKEVEN POINT

Now let's get back to The Breakeven Point and understand what that concept is about.

The concept of Break-Even analysis originated a long time ago with very large companies who had factories that specialized in making one product. It was easy for them to figure out how many units of widgets (or whatever they were making) they needed to produce in order to get to that magic land called profitability.

I first encountered this concept in my cost accounting class in college. After that class, I thought to myself, "*Wow, that was interesting! Now, I wonder if they have German beer for one dollar at the campus Rathskeller tonight*?" (Yes ladies and gentlemen, this is exactly how college students think.)

The next time I encountered it was in my training to become a Merchant Banker. I thought that it was strange that this had come back into my life to be part of my investment banking training. But I think that the reason is because back in those days, banking was a relationship-based business. You evaluated your client's profitability for the long term. True, there were many deals that were purely transactional. But to a British bank – in those days – your reputation as an underwriter was of paramount importance. And we needed to know that whatever deals we made were absolutely blue-chip.

And it is strange that out of everything we learned, this is the concept that stuck to me the longest. I just love it! (Yes. I am a nurd. What did you expect?)

Anyway, The Break-Even Point, or Break-Even Analysis is a fundamental concept in the quest for company to be profitable. Then to go beyond that and to be more profitable than your competition.

Once again, the breakeven point is defined as:

That point in your profit and loss where all your income is the same as all of your expenses so that your net profit is zero. And (here is the good part), that in turn means you have now covered ALL of your expenses and thus, your next dollar of revenue (or sales) is 100% profit.

Sweet!

But let's put some numbers to the idea. Let's say that your monthly rent is $1,500 a month. How many apple turnovers will you need to make and sell to pay that rent? The answer obviously is at least 1,000 because you sell each apple turnover for $1.50. But remember that your rent needs to be paid in advance. Which means that you will have to make about 1,000 apple turnovers to cover next month's rent.

But we know that it costs us money in terms of labor and raw material to make each and every one of those apple turnovers. Which means that in order to pay the rent we are going to have to make more than just 1,000 apple turnovers.

The question is, how many?

The concept of break-even analysis is to give us exactly that answer. It will tell us exactly how many apple turnovers we have to make in order to cover all of our expenses. Because once we have covered all of our expenses then the very next apple turnover that we make will give us 100% profit.

However,

We have a complication in that Mom's Bakery sells more than apple turnovers. They also sell, cakes, pastries, coffee, etc. Therefore, we will learn to perform our Break-Even Analysis not based on number of units sold of the apple turnovers, but in terms of dollars.

When we have a mix of products we can, if we wish, breakdown each product into an individual cost stream and then segment out the revenue associated with that product in order to get the Break-Even point for each product sold.

But that is a complicated endeavor and beyond the scope of this narrative.

When we have a small business, we just need to know if we are going to be profitable or not. And if so, when?

The first step is to break down our expenses into two categories:

1. *Variable Expenses*: A broad definition of this is all of the expenses that go into making each unit of your finished product in which the cost for this category varies depending on how many you make. The main idea of what makes a variable expense variable is that the expense varies in direct

relation with the number of units produced. So, for example, the more apple turnovers you make the more you will have to pay for labor and flour. Thus, raw materials and direct labor are variable expenses.

But let's look closer at this; for example, if in one hour you can produce 100 turnovers and it costs you $15 an hour to pay two bakers to make those 100 turnovers (say that minimum wage is $7.50 an hour – yeah, those were the days, right?) Then your cost to produce EACH turnover is $15/100 = .15 cents per turnover just for the bakers (direct **labor** cost). Let us also say that the cost of materials (flour, eggs, shortening, etc.) for each turnover is another .15 cents (direct **material** cost). If you add those two together, then your cost to make each turnover is .30 cents an hour.
If you produce no turnovers because your bakers are out to lunch then your labor cost as well as material costs for that hour is -0-.

Other example of variable costs are:

a. Raw inventory: In this case flour, eggs, shortening, etc.
b. Hourly wages of other people directly involved in making the product.
c. Other costs involved in the making of the product. Such as electricity and other utilities. (This is called Manufacturing Overhead and is calculated separately from labor and materials).

2. *Fixed Expenses*: These are expenses that do not vary with manufacturing. Such as for example, rent, payments on the leased equipment used to manufacture the product (ovens,

mixers, etc.) or the wages of the manufacturing supervisor (if he or she is on a salary).

If for example, your monthly rent is $1,500 a month and this is September then that means that your daily rent is $1,500/30 days = $50 a day. If your shop is open for eight hours then that rental cost becomes $50/8 hours = $6.25 an hour.

If you produce NO turnovers in that hour then your rental cost for that hour is still $6.25 an hour. If, on the other hand, you produce 100 turnovers in that hour then your rental cost is still $6.25 an hour or $6.25/100, which is about .06 cents per turnover. Therefore, if you produce no turnovers then your hourly cost of rent is $6.25. But if you produce 100 turnovers in that hour then your hourly cost for rent is now only .06 cents.

If, however, you only produce 50 turnovers in that hour then your rental costs is still $6.25 an hour but since you only produced on 50 turnovers instead of 100 then your rental cost per turnover has now gone up to $6.25/50 = which is about .13 cents an hour.

Because you have produced less turnovers your rental cost has doubled as measured per turnover.

Now some people may argue that because the cost of the rent varies with the number of turnovers produced that makes this a variable cost also. (As shown above).

But there is a difference as to being a cost that is DIRECTLY influenced by the units of production and a cost that is INDIRECTLY influenced by the units of production. Variable costs are directly influenced by units of production. Fixed costs are indirectly influenced by the units of production.

Evidently, the secret to profitability is to make as many turnovers as possible in an hour to shrink those fixed costs per hour. For example, if you manage to make 200 turnovers in that hour instead of 100 then your fixed rental costs of $6.25 per hour go down to about .03 cents an hour ($6.25/200 = .03).

So,

Your Variable Costs will move up or down based on how many units (turnovers) you make.

Your Fixed Costs don't change at all. If you close the shop to go on vacation and produce nothing you will still have to pay those fixed costs.

But here is the thing: the secret to success:
Ready?

The secret to success is to balance manufacturing as many units as you can per a given timeframe (i.e., an hour) WHILE MAINTAINING PRODUCT QUALITY.

And if we want to be philosophical – that is, what the secret of life is? It is balancing things out. Or Aristotle's "Golden Mean."

You may also find that you can reduce your expenses by how you manage your variable expenses. You may, for example, find that you can get a lower price for your raw materials – in this case, let us use flour for the turnovers as an example.

The lower cost may have instant benefits in the short run – namely – lower cost of manufacturing the product, which means higher profits.

But there may be hidden costs. If the lower priced flour is of lower quality you may have an increased percentage of bad product quality. Which means that while in the short run your profit will be higher, in the long run, you may have dissatisfied customers which will lead to lower revenue and lower profits in the long run.

This is a problem in the manufacturing industry where substandard products are rejected by the Quality Assurance Department or by the customer. They usually have to be disposed of or reworked. This results in waste and extra costs.

What is the answer?

There is no hard and fast answer. All companies struggle with this dilemma on a daily basis. From the Fortune 500 corporations to the guy on the street corner selling hot dogs out of a pushcart.

But as you grow your business this is what you should concentrate on:

Concentrate on building market share.

Whether you have lots of competition or none – build market share.

Why? Because there is a certain critical mass – in terms of revenue – which, when you reach it will on its own momentum launch your product into higher sales and profit.

Your job is to get to that critical mass. This is like a snowball rolling downhill. It will eventually get to the point where it is very difficult to stop. Because it is carried forward on its own momentum.

You get to that critical mass by excellent product and service.

AND: Please note, this does not mean that you must solely concentrate on building market share to the exclusion of all else. Yes, you must also focus on profitability and cash flow. But building market share comes first.

Come on! If this stuff was simple it would not be any fun at all!

Back to Breakeven Analysis:

To summarize, in breakeven analysis you have two kinds of expenses: variable and fixed. Variable expenses will vary with the number of units produced. If you produce zero units then your variable expenses will be zero.

Fixed expenses stay the same and must be paid whether you produce any units or not. That monthly rent will have to be paid even if you close shop for that month.

Now, we get to put all of this together in a few easy steps.

1. Make a list of all Variable Expenses. (Total Variable Expenses.)
2. Make a list of all Fixed Expenses. (Total Fixed Expenses.)
3. Subtract your Variable Expenses from your Net Revenues (Revenues less Returns and Allowances).
4. Step three will give you what is called a Contribution Margin. (Very different from Gross Margin.)
5. Divide your Contribution Margin by your Net Revenues. This will give you a percentage named Contribution Margin Ratio.
6. Divide your Total Fixed Expenses by your Contribution Margin Ratio.
7. This will give you what you are looking for and that is our Breakeven Volume. That is to say your - Breakeven Volume in Sales.

Let's jump into an example:

First, we will need that income statement that we were looking at a few pages back.

REVENUE	in $	In %	
Gross Sales	$ 267,010	100%	
Less Customer Discounts	$ (561)	0%	IGNORE
NET SALES	$ 266,449	100%	
COST OF GOODS SOLD			
Beginning Inventory	$ 3,256	1%	
Purchases	$ 76,000	28%	
Less Ending Inventory	$ (2,358)	-1%	
COST OF GOODS AVAILABLE for SALE	$ 76,898	29%	VARIABLE
Production Direct Labor	$ 63,510	24%	VARIABLE
Production Depreciation	$ 3,000	1%	
Production Overhead	$ 3,000	1%	???
TOTAL COST of GOODS SOLD	$ 146,408	55%	
GROSS PROFIT	$ 120,041	45%	
SALES, GENERAL & OPERATING EXPENSES			
Advertising	$ 356	0%	IGNORE
Counter Sales Salaries & Wages	$ 65,850	25%	VARIABLE
Rent	$ 18,000	7%	
Supplies	$ 12,575	5%	VARIABLE
Maintenance	$ 79	0%	IGNORE
Utilities	$ 596	0%	IGNORE
Depreciation - Store	$ 2,000	1%	
Miscellaneous	$ 287	0%	IGNORE
TOTAL SALES, GENERAL & OPERATING EXPENSES	$ 99,743	37%	
NET PROFIT	$ 20,298	8%	

I have gone ahead and indicated which items are variable and which items are not. Those items which are 0% we can ignore. The reality is that they are somewhere in the less than .1% category, but the system rounds them to zero. However, they are sufficiently small, which makes them immaterial. Nor are they, in aggregate, material. Finance and accounting is not about being perfectly accurate. It is about being reasonably accurate. You will find out why in the Pricing Section of this book.

You will notice that I have indicated that the Counter Sales Salaries & Wages, is variable. That is because, despite the name, all of these employees are in fact, hourly. It would be different if they were salaried. In that case they would be a fixed expense. And, if some of them were salaried and others hourly we would have to break out the salaried from the hourly before we can continue our analysis.

Production overhead (pointed out by the black arrow with question marks), can be either Variable or Fixed depending on the nature of the expense. For example, if a manufacturing company has a warehouse manager who is salaried then this would be a fixed expense in the Overhead category. On the other hand, the shipping clerk in the same warehouse (receives and sends out inventory) would be hourly and that would be a variable expense also in the Overhead Category. In this case, Production Overhead consists of the utility expenses for the kitchen as well as the kitchen's share of the property taxes for the building. Now Property taxes don't really change much. And Utilities, although they can fluctuate in small amounts are usually within a set range. Therefore, for this example, this is a fixed expense. I say for this example because different companies experience costs differently.

Everything else which is not Variable is then a Fixed Expense. Pretty simple, actually.

The next step is to segment the Revenue, Variable Expenses and Fixed Expenses into a new format. It would be as follows:

MOM's BAKERY - BREAK EVEN ANALYSIS

REVENUE	in $	In %
Gross Sales	$ 267,010	100%
Less Customer Discounts	$ (561)	0%
NET SALES	$ 266,449	100%
VARIABLE EXPENSES		
Cost of Goods Available for Sale	$ 76,898	29%
Production Direct Labor	$ 63,510	24%
Counter Sales Salaries & Wages	$ 65,850	25%
Supplies	$ 12,575	5%
TOTAL VARIABLE	$ 218,833	82%
CONTRIBUTION MARGIN	$ 47,616	18%
FIXED EXPENSES		
Rent	$ 18,000	7%
Depreciation - Store	$ 2,000	1%
Production Depreciation	$ 3,000	1%
Production Overhead	$ 3,000	1%
Plug	$ 1,318	0%
TOTAL FIXED EXPENSES	$ 27,318 a	10%
NET PROFIT	$ 20,298	8%
	$ -	
BREAK EVEN CALCULATION		
Total Fixed Expenses	$ 27,318	
DIVIDED BY: Contribution Margin	18%	
EQUALS BREAKEVEN VOLUME in $	$ 151,767 d	a/b=d
DAILY REVENUE	$ 267,010	
Divided by Days in Year	365	
Equals daily Sales	$ 732 e	
Days to Break Even =d/e	207	209 Days is about 7 Months.

Take the NET REVENUE (NET SALES) and subtract the Total Variable Expenses from it. The remainder is your Contribution Margin of $47,616.

Then divide your Contribution Margin (the $47,616) by the Net Revenue (Sales) to get it as a percentage. In this case it is 18%. (i.e. $47,616/$266,449 = 18%)

Finally, divide your Total Fixed Expenses by the Contribution Margin Ratio (the 18%.)

$$\$27,318/ 18\% = \$151,767$$

That $151,767 is the amount in sales that you need to make over the course of the year in order to cover all of your expenses. In other words, to have a net profit of zero. Every dollar in sales that you make after that is 100% profit.

You may, if you wish, take one more step. You may want to find out what your Breakeven point is in terms of time. In this case, since we calculated the Break Even point for one year we can see how long it will take during that year to get to this point.

Divide you Net Revenue by the number of days in the year:

$$\$266,464 / 365 = \$732 \text{ a day.}$$

Now just divide your Breakeven Volume by the $732:

$$\$151,767 / \$732 = 207 \text{ days.}$$

Which means that it takes Mom's Bakery about seven months to Break Even. After that point all of your expenses for the year are covered and it is smooth sailing until New Year's Eve. In other words, you have about five months of pure profitability.

Why do we need to know this?
We need to use this tool in order to make good business decisions. Should we hire another baker? Can we raise our prices? Can we drop our prices?

All important questions that you will have to face if you are to run your own business. Hopefully, you now have a new tool in your toolbox to help you navigate being a business owner.

Note: Some of you may wonder why we can't plug the $151,767 (the Break-Even Volume) into the income statement in order to see if our Net Profit will end up at zero.

That will not work. The problem is your Variable Expenses. With a Sales Volume of only $151,767 versus $266,464 your variable expenses would be a lot less. What that would be we can find out if we do ratio analysis.

But that is for another course.

The last observation is that we have done this analysis for one year. We can easily do it for one month. In fact, my normal way to manage the finance department of any business that I worked for was to do it monthly then compare it to the previous month(s). If my Breakeven point had gone up I knew that I had a problem. If my Break-Even point had gone down. Then life was good.

Miller time!

What we have just done is representative of an ideal world. Let's change the numbers a little bit to see what happens in a less than ideal world.

REVENUE	in $	In %
Gross Sales	$ 267,010	100%
Less Customer Discounts	$ (561)	0%
NET SALES	**$ 266,449**	**100%**
COST OF GOODS SOLD		
Beginning Inventory	$ 3,256	1%
Purchases	$ 76,000	28%
Less Ending Inventory	$ (2,358)	-1%
COST OF GOODS AVAILABLE for SALE	$ 76,898	29%
Production Direct Labor	$ 85,000	32%
Production Depreciation	$ 3,000	1%
Production Overhead	$ 3,000	1%
TOTAL COST of GOODS SOLD	**$ 167,898**	**63%**
GROSS PROFIT	**$ 98,551**	**37%**
SALES, GENERAL & OPERATING EXPENSES		
Advertising	$ 356	0%
Counter Sales Salaries & Wages	$ 70,000	26%
Rent	$ 18,000	7%
Supplies	$ 12,575	5%
Maintenance	$ 79	0%
Utilities	$ 596	0%
Depreciation - Store	$ 2,000	1%
Miscellaneous	$ 287	0%
TOTAL SALES, GENERAL & OPERATING EXPENSES	**$ 103,893**	**39%**
NET PROFIT	**$ (5,342)**	**-2%**

In the above scenario we have changed two numbers – the, Production Direct Labor has been increased to $85,000 and the, Counter Sales Salaries & Wages, has been increased to $70,000.

All the other numbers remain the same.

And, as you can see, instead of a Net Profit of $20,298 we now have a Net Loss of -$5,342.

What can we do about it?
In this case we can do one of two things: Increase sales volume (sell more apple turnovers as well as anything else you can get your hands on.) Or, you can raise prices. Ideally you would be able to do both. However, raising prices is a very delicate thing because you might lose a few customers.

Let us say however, that Mom's Bakery was able to do both – increase sales volume and marginally raise prices. What would be the result?

REVENUE	in $	In %
Gross Sales	$ 300,000	100%
Less Customer Discounts	$ (561)	0%
NET SALES	$ 299,439	112%
COST OF GOODS SOLD		
Beginning Inventory	$ 3,256	1%
Purchases	$ 76,000	28%
Less Ending Inventory	$ (2,358)	-1%
COST OF GOODS AVAILABLE for SALE	$ 76,898	29%
Production Direct Labor	$ 85,000	32%
Production Depreciation	$ 3,000	1%
Production Overhead	$ 3,000	1%
TOTAL COST of GOODS SOLD	$ 167,898	63%
GROSS PROFIT	$ 131,541	49%
SALES, GENERAL & OPERATING EXPENSES		
Advertising	$ 356	0%
Counter Sales Salaries & Wages	$ 70,000	26%
Rent	$ 18,000	7%
Supplies	$ 12,575	5%
Maintenance	$ 79	0%
Utilities	$ 596	0%
Depreciation - Store	$ 2,000	1%
Miscellaneous	$ 287	0%
TOTAL SALES, GENERAL & OPERATING EXPENSES	$ 103,893	39%
NET PROFIT	$ 27,648	10%

As you can see, if we raise sales revenue to $300,000 our -$5,342 loss will become a $27,648 gain.

Let's look at one more scenario (just for giggles.)

In the below example we have a Net Profit of negative -$135,192. Not good at all.

Question is, how can we fix this? The problem here is that the Gross Profit – instead of being positive is NEGATIVE. This is very bad stuff. Because it means that Mom's Bakery is selling her merchandise for LESS THAN THE COST TO MAKE IT. It is as if an auto maker sells a brand-new car for $1,000 when it cost $5,000 to manufacture it.

Increasing sales volume will not help. In fact, the more she sells the more money she will lose. The only way to fix this is to raise the prices of what she sells. Which is a difficult thing to do. Lately, I have seen this sort of situation in publicly traded companies. In my day we would never have a company go public with a negative Gross Profit. Because in that case, their Break-Even Point is infinity, and they will never see a net profit or any sort of profitability at all. If you see a publicly traded company that has this unfortunate characteristic then do not buy their stock. These companies only stay afloat because they sell equity to the public. To me, they are money pits.

REVENUE		in $	In %
Gross Sales	$	267,010	100%
Less Customer Discounts	$	(561)	0%
NET SALES	$	266,449	100%
COST OF GOODS SOLD			
Beginning Inventory	$	3,256	1%
Purchases	$	**95,000**	36%
Less Ending Inventory	$	(2,358)	-1%
COST OF GOODS AVAILABLE for SALE	$	95,898	36%
Production Direct Labor	$	**200,000**	75%
Production Depreciation	$	3,000	1%
Production Overhead	$	3,000	1%
TOTAL COST of GOODS SOLD	$	301,898	113%
GROSS PROFIT	$	(35,449)	-13%
SALES, GENERAL & OPERATING EXPENSES			
Advertising	$	356	0%
Counter Sales Salaries & Wages	$	65,850	25%
Rent	$	18,000	7%
Supplies	$	12,575	5%
Maintenance	$	79	0%
Utilities	$	596	0%
Depreciation - Store	$	2,000	1%
Miscellaneous	$	287	0%
TOTAL SALES, GENERAL & OPERATING EXPENSES	$	99,743	37%
NET PROFIT	$	(135,192)	-51%

PRODUCT PRICING

Now comes the trickiest part of starting and running your business. And that is pricing your product. If you set the price too high not many people will buy it. If you set the price too low, people will buy it, but you will be giving away profit.

There are three steps to pricing a product.

Step 1. Find out what the total cost is.

Step 2. Investigate the market for the product.

Step 3. Set the initial price.

The hardest step is the first one. This in itself can be broken down into three steps.

Step 1. Find out your direct costs in material.

Step 2. Find out your direct costs in labor to transform the material into finished goods ready for sale.

Step 4. Find out what the overhead is to manufacture these goods.

Step 5. Find out what other costs are involved in the direct manufacture of the product and allocate these costs.

Step 6. Add up all the costs into a spreadsheet. I mention this because product costs are not static. They will change over time. If you have this all organized into a spreadsheet then when the time comes to change something all you need to do is change the numbers that have increased (or decreased).

Step 7. Add in the markup. The markup is the amount of profit that you add into your product on top of all the costs. So, for example, if after all of the work mentioned above is done and Mom's Bakery finds out that it costs her $3.50 to make each apple turnover and she wants to make a profit of $1.50 then she will mark the apple turnovers up by $1.50. Which means that the selling price of each apple turnover is $5.00. Markup is usually expressed in terms of percentage. In this case the markup would be 43%, which is $1.50 / $3.50 = 43%

Find What the Total Cost is

Direct Costs of Materials: We will continue to use Mom's Bakery for our examples. In this case the costs of the materials are as follows:

COST of MATERIALS in BULK		Amount USED	COST of MATERIALS per Batch
1lb of flour	$ 3.00	1/2	$ 1.50
Dozen Eggs	$ 3.50	One Egg	$ 0.29
Milk	$ 2.00	1/4	$ 0.50
Lb of Sugar	$ 2.30	1/4	$ 0.58
1 Lb Frozen Apples	$ 2.50	Entire Package	$ 2.50
1 Package of Yeast	$ 0.50	Entire Package	$ 0.50
	$ 13.80	Cost of Batch	$ 5.87
		Cost of Each Apple Turnover	$ 0.49

On the left-hand side is the cost of purchasing these materials *in bulk*. (You can't go to the store and just buy one egg or a cup of sugar). On the right-hand side is the cost of these materials that were purchased in bulk broken down into the cost of what it takes to make a dozen apple turnovers. We make a dozen apple turnovers at a time because it is more cost effective to make a large amount – such as a dozen – than an individual amount. If Mom's Bakery were to make 24 turnovers at a time (in other words – at a batch), rather than only a dozen it would be even more cost effective. The amount of material (in bulk cost), would be the same but the labor hours to produce them would be more cost effective. However, for this illustration we will just make a dozen at a time.

Now we see that the cost to make each turnover is only .49 cents in terms of material.

Direct Costs of Labor:

Let us say, that in order for Mom's Bakery to make the batch of apple turnovers she will use one baker and that it will take him/her about 30 minutes to make each batch. It actually takes an hour to make a batch of apple turnovers, but not all of this time is spent on actually making them. Once you mix the flour, yeast, milk, and the egg then you have to wait for the yeast to make the dough rise. Usually, it takes half an hour for that to happen. When that is done you take the dough and shape it then put in the apple mixture (chopped apples, sugar, etc.). Once that is done you put the turnovers in the oven. And wait 30 minutes until they are baked. Therefore, there is a lot of waiting involved in making the turnovers. Rather than stand around doing nothing the baker will start on the next batch of turnovers or will perform another task. But, in the final analysis, the time it takes the baker to use his/her hands to actually create the batch is only ½ hour. If we are paying each baker $7.50 an hour to make a dozen turnovers then our labor cost is $3.75 a 1/2 hour. Which means that the labor cost of each turnover is about .31 cents ($3.75 / 12 = .31)

But that is only direct labor costs. We also need to factor in the Burden. The burden is any other cost related to labor that is not a wage. So, for example, the employer mandated payment on FICA and Medicare, vacation time, health benefits, etc.

The current employer tax rate for FICA is 6.2% and for Medicare it is 1.45%. Which means that the employer pays 7.65%. If we apply this to the .31 cents that is the wage expense for each turnover we get

.31 cents x 7.65% = .02 cents. But let us also say that other benefits such as vacation and health benefits are $1.65 per employee per hour. (This would be an average because the rate for each employee is different. Some employees have more vacation than others based on seniority and have more expensive health benefits based on age). If we divide the $1.65 by half (remember – it only takes ½ hour to make a turnover) then the amount is .83 cents per dozen turnovers. If we divide the .83 cents by 12 we get .07 cents per turnover.

Now we have a pretty good idea of what our labor costs are per turnover. As follows:

$	0.31	Direct Wages
$	0.02	FICA & Medicare
$	0.07	Other Burden: Benefits
$	0.40	TOTAL LABOR COSTS

Overhead:

Overhead is defined as anything that is related to producing and selling a product besides direct material and direct labor.

There are two types of Overhead, and they are Manufacturing Overhead and Non-Manufacturing Overhead (also known as MG&A which stands for Management, General and Administrative Expenses).

We will start with Manufacturing Overhead. In Manufacturing Overhead there are also two types, and these are Fixed and Variable. As follows:

Fixed Overhead: Is any overhead directly related to manufacturing and which is at a fixed dollar amount. This includes depreciation on machinery, rent on the production facility (the kitchen), the salary of the manufacturing supervisor and the salary of the warehouse manager (if you have one).

Variable Overhead: Is any overhead that varies with the level of production. In our example, the more apple turnovers that Mom's bakery makes then the higher the cost of this overhead. In this example we will include utilities such as electricity and water. (Remember that Manufacturing Overhead is anything related to making the product which is not material and labor). Also, the cost of, freight-in, which is the cost of delivery of material to the kitchen.

Let us work with an example.

First, we are going to break out the Fixed Manufacturing Overhead expenses:

The first step is to separate what we make in the kitchen as opposed to what we buy then resell. What we make in the kitchen is limited to: Apple Turnovers, Custom Cakes and Other Pastries. The other things we sell such as juices we buy from another company in ready to sell inventory then simply stock it and sell it with a markup. Coffee we do make in house, but it is not made in the kitchen. It is made in the shop by the counter people.

We can see that apple turnovers make up $54,750 out of the total $267,010 in our yearly revenue. That is 21% of yearly revenue. In similar fashion, custom cakes is 1% of our yearly revenue and Other pastries, (eclairs, muffins, etc.) is 9% of our yearly revenue.

But now we need to isolate these numbers and sales items into what we ONLY MAKE IN THE KITCHEN. (You will see why in a minute).

What we only make in the kitchen are three sales items: Apple Turnovers, Custom Cakes and Other Pastries.

Out of the total $267,010 of our gross revenue the sale of these three items is $80,510. Apple turnovers, in terms of revenue, makes up $54,750 out of the total $80,510. In other words, apple turnovers make up 68% of kitchen revenues.

Therefore, we will make an assumption that apple turnovers also constitute 68% of the kitchen expenses.

Apple Turnovers	$ 54,750	21%
Coffee	$ 146,000	55%
Custom Cakes	$ 2,400	1%
Other Pastries	$ 23,360	9%
Juices	$ 36,500	14%
Other Stuff	$ 4,000	1%
	$ 267,010	100%

Apple Turnovers	$ 54,750	68%
Custom Cakes	$ 2,400	3%
Other Pastries	$ 23,360	29%
	$ 80,510	100%

Now let us look at some of those expenses to see how we can allocate the overhead costs.

Fixed Overhead:

Depreciation: $3,000 a year or $250 a month

Rent: $18,000 a year for the entire building of which the kitchen is half of the building.

    This is then, $18,000 / 2 = $9,000 A year rent expense for the kitchen alone.

    Which then is $9,000 /12 = $750 a month for the kitchen rent.

Total Fixed Overhead is then:

Depreciation: $250

Rent: $750
TOTAL $1,000

Variable Overhead:

Earlier in this book we decided that Mom's Bakery does not have any fixed Overhead in the kitchen. Certainly, in some cases (for example) utilities would be a variable overhead. If you have for example a company that uses an electric smelter as part of producing goods then that would be a variable overhead expense. Electric smelters are expensive to run. Therefore, they are only turned on when producing stuff. In a bakery however, the ovens are left on all day long since production is continuous. And that gives us a fairly consistent electric bill. This rule is not set in stone. You will have to make a determination for your business based on how you produce your inventory. For this book we will say that the $3,000 of production overhead is actually fixed.

Therefore, we will call it, Other Fixed Overhead, (just for this exercise):

Other Fixed Overhead:

Property taxes and utilities: $3,000 a year is then $3,000 / 12 = $250 a month.

We can now create an analysis of the cost of Overhead per turnover as follows: (Remember that Mom's Bakery sells 100 turnovers a day. Which means that she makes 100 turnovers a day).

APPLE TURNOVER OVERHEAD ALLOCATION	Per Year	Per Month	Per Turnover (100 a day)
Depreciation	$ 3,000.00	$ 250.00	$ 0.08
Rent	$ 9,000.00	$ 750.00	$ 0.25
Variable Overhead	$ -	$ -	$ -
Other Fixed Overhead	$ 3,000.00	$ 250.00	$ 0.08
TOTAL Overhead	$ 15,000.00	$ 1,250.00	$ 0.42

We can now add all of the costs together to find out how much it costs us to create each apple turnover from all of the work that we have done in the preceding pages. Also, we have been using a dozen turnovers to calculate our costs per turnover. Yet in overhead we used 100 turnovers. But the end result is that our basis is still per turnover.

Cost of Materials: (From Page 50)

COST of MATERIALS in BULK		Amount USED	COST of MATERIALS per Batch
1lb of flour	$ 3.00	1/2	$ 1.50
Dozen Eggs	$ 3.50	One Egg	$ 0.29
Milk	$ 2.00	1/4	$ 0.50
Lb of Sugar	$ 2.30	1/4	$ 0.58
1 Lb Frozen Apples	$ 2.50	Entire Package	$ 2.50
1 Package of Yeast	$ 0.50	Entire Package	$ 0.50
	$ 13.80	Cost of Batch	$ 5.87
		Cost of Each Apple Turnover	$ 0.49

Cost of Labor: (From Page 52)

$	0.31	Direct Wages
$	0.02	FICA & Medicare
$	0.07	Other Burden: Benefits
$	0.40	TOTAL LABOR COSTS

Cost of Overhead: (From previous page)

APPLE TURNOVER OVERHEAD ALLOCATION	Per Year	Per Month	Per Turnover (100 a day)
Depreciation	$ 3,000.00	$ 250.00	$ 0.08
Rent	$ 9,000.00	$ 750.00	$ 0.25
Variable Overhead	$ -	$ -	$ -
Other Fixed Overhead	$ 3,000.00	$ 250.00	$ 0.08
TOTAL Overhead	$ 15,000.00	$ 1,250.00	$ 0.42

And when we add all of those up we get:

COST TO PRODUCE EACH APPLE TURNOVER	
Cost of Material:	$ 0.49
Cost of Labor:	$ 0.40
Cost of Overhead:	$ 0.42
Total Costs to Produce	$ 1.31
Sales Price per Turnover	$1.50
Profit Margin per Turnover	$0.19

So, it costs us approximately $1.31 to create each apple turnover and we sell them for $1.50 each. That gives us a profit margin of .19 cents per turnover. Not very profitable is it? If we sell 100 of these a day then that gives us a profit of $19 a day or $19 a day times 365 days a year = $6,935. (Approximately – yes, you will hear this word a lot in finance and accounting).

But remember that the $1.31 is only the cost to produce the turnovers – not to sell them. We still have to look at those expenses.

If we go back to page 54 we can see the breakdown of everything we sell as compared to just what we sell and that is made in our kitchen. The same breakdown is shown below. If you will remember, we needed to break out the overhead in the kitchen only so that we could apply it to the kitchen overhead to find out what that was per apple turnover.

Apple Turnovers	$ 54,750	21%
Coffee	$ 146,000	55%
Custom Cakes	$ 2,400	1%
Other Pastries	$ 23,360	9%
Juices	$ 36,500	14%
Other Stuff	$ 4,000	1%
	$ 267,010	100%

Apple Turnovers	$ 54,750	68%
Custom Cakes	$ 2,400	3%
Other Pastries	$ 23,360	29%
	$ 80,510	100%

That is the bottom part of the analysis that only has the Apple Turnovers, Custom Cakes and Other Pastries.

But now that we are going to examine the overhead of the selling area we have to take everything that we sell into consideration. Therefore, we will use the top half of the analysis. The long breakout that starts with Apple Turnovers and ends with Other Stuff.

Apple Turnovers	$ 54,750	21%
Coffee	$ 146,000	55%
Custom Cakes	$ 2,400	1%
Other Pastries	$ 23,360	9%
Juices	$ 36,500	14%
Other Stuff	$ 4,000	1%
	$ 267,010	100%

As before, we can see that Apple Turnovers make up 21% of everything that we sell in the store. Therefore, we will use that 21% to calculate the amount of overhead expenses in the store that we need to apply to the Apple Turnovers.

Let us go back to the income statement that we originally looked at way back in page 18 of this book.

When we broke out all of the expenses that are involved in manufacturing the Apple Turnovers. That is the top half of the income statement up to the line that says, "TOTAL COST of GOODS SOLD". (Shown below).

MOM'S BAKERY INCOME STATEMENT – TWELVE MONTHS ENDED 20XX

REVENUE	in $	In %
Gross Sales	$ 267,010	100%
Less Customer Discounts	$ (561)	0%
NET SALES	$ 266,449	100%
COST OF GOODS SOLD		
Beginning Inventory	$ 3,256	1%
Purchases	$ 76,000	28%
Less Ending Inventory	$ (2,358)	-1%
COST OF GOODS AVAILABLE for SALE	$ 76,898	29%
Production Direct Labor	$ 63,510	24%
Production Depreciation	$ 3,000	1%
Production Overhead	$ 3,000	1%
TOTAL COST of GOODS SOLD	$ 146,408	55%

But additionally, we added the part of the rent that applies to the kitchen as part of that breakout.

The total rent for the building was in the section called, "TOTAL SALES, GENERAL AND ADMINISTRATIVE EXPENSES". And it was – as shown below – a total of $18,000 for the year.

MOM'S BAKERY INCOME STATEMENT – TWELVE MONTHS ENDED 20XX

REVENUE		in $	In %
Gross Sales	$	267,010	100%
Less Customer Discounts	$	(561)	0%
NET SALES	$	266,449	100%
COST OF GOODS SOLD			
Beginning Inventory	$	3,256	1%
Purchases	$	76,000	28%
Less Ending Inventory	$	(2,358)	-1%
COST OF GOODS AVAILABLE for SALE	$	76,898	29%
Production Direct Labor	$	63,510	24%
Production Depreciation	$	3,000	1%
Production Overhead	$	3,000	1%
TOTAL COST of GOODS SOLD	$	146,408	55%
GROSS PROFIT	$	120,041	45%
SALES, GENERAL & OPERATING EXPENSES			
Advertising	$	356	0%
Counter Sales Salaries & Wages	$	65,850	25%
Rent	$	18,000	7%
Supplies	$	12,575	5%
Maintenance	$	79	0%
Utilities	$	596	0%
Depreciation - Store	$	2,000	1%
Miscellaneous	$	287	0%
TOTAL SALES, GENERAL & OPERATING EXPENSES	$	99,743	37%
NET PROFIT	$	20,298	8%

But half of that $18,000 was for the kitchen. Therefore, if we only want to isolate the expenses for the store then we need to change how that bottom half of the income statement looks.

SALES, GENERAL & OPERATING EXPENSES			
Advertising	$	356	0%
Counter Sales Salaries & Wages	$	65,850	25%
Rent	$	9,000	3%
Supplies	$	12,575	5%
Maintenance	$	79	0%
Utilities	$	596	0%
Depreciation - Store	$	2,000	1%
Miscellaneous	$	287	0%
TOTAL SALES, GENERAL & OPERATING EXPENSES	$	90,743	34%

As seen above, we have changed the rent amount to $9,000 and now we can proceed to calculate the overhead for the store.

Now our job becomes relatively easier because we have previously isolated the costs for just the kitchen and in doing so we also isolated the costs for just the store which are $90,743 for the year. Given the fact that the Apple Turnovers are 21% of the store sales (therefore 21% of the expenses) then the total cost of selling just the Apple Turnovers becomes $19,056 for the year.

$	90,743
	21%
$	19,056

If we calculate that we sell 100 Apple Turnovers a day that is 36,500 Apple Turnovers a year. Then, to figure out how much it costs to just sell every Apple Turnover all we have to do is divide the $19,056 by the 36,500 and we get .52 cents. Now we have an understanding of the complete cost of making AND selling each Apple Turnover.

COST TO PRODUCE EACH APPLE TURNOVER		
Cost of Material:	$	0.49
Cost of Labor:	$	0.40
Cost of Overhead:	$	0.42
Total Costs to Produce	$	1.31
Sales Price per Turnover		$1.50
Profit Margin per Turnover		$0.19

Remember that it cost us $1,31 to make each turnover. If then, in addition to that, it costs us an extra .52 to sell each Apple Turnover then we are actually losing money every time we sell an Apple Turnover as shown below:

COST TO PRODUCE EACH APPLE TURNOVER		
Cost of Material:	$	0.49
Cost of Labor:	$	0.40
Cost of Overhead:	$	0.42
Total Costs to Produce	$	1.31
Total Cost to Sell Each Apple Trunover	$	0.52
Total Cost (Making and Selling):	$	1.83
Sales Price per Turnover		$1.50
Profit Margin per Turnover		($0.33)

Therefore, when we calculate the costs to actually make AND sell each Apple Turnover it turns out that we are losing .33 each time we put one into the customers' hands.

How can this happen you ask? It happens. It happens a lot.

And the reason this happens is because <u>companies do not know how to calculate the cost of putting a product into the customer's hands</u>. That is the ultimate objective of our exercise. You would be surprised how many sophisticated and successful companies do not know how much money it costs them to put a product in the hands of the customer. Most companies (even Fortune 500 companies) focus on the Gross Profit. Then they manage their net profit by cutting costs in the SG&A section. (Layoff support people such as marketing, accounting, product support and quality assurance.) There have been many times when I have been told that I needed to let people in my department go because, "We need to start doing more with less."

Which resulted in many very talented as well as qualified people leaving. People get stressed and go to greener pastures, (including myself). This is the way many companies manage net profit. And it works in the short run. In the long run quality erodes and customers go buy their products somewhere else. At that point, these companies start bringing in more people and absorbing the loss to shore up eroding sales and client base. Then the cycle starts all over again. Pretty sad isn't it?

I developed this technique when I was working for a company in the aerospace industry. They had a very good gross profit of 55% which they were very proud of. But they had negative net profit. How can that be? Well, they did not know how to price their products correctly. As I mentioned before, they needed to understand how to price the total cost of their products by <u>how much it costs to put their products into the customers hands.</u>

Back to our problem, if then, we are selling our Apple Turnovers at a loss how is it possible that we made a $20,298 net profit for the year?

Because we sell a mixture of other things. Some of them are overpriced and some of them are underpriced (the Apple Turnovers are definitely underpriced). The mixture of sales items creates a net profit of $20,298. The point that I am trying to make, however, is that the net profit could be a lot higher if we truly understood the cost/profitability dynamic for every item we sell.

The other thing that needs to be pointed out is that it is a good thing that we only sold 36,500 Apple Turnovers for the year. Because if we had sold more our net profit would have been less. In other words, the more apple turnovers she makes the less net profit she will experience. Because in a composite product mix as Mom's Bakery has, some products will crowd out the other ones. And perhaps, the unprofitable products will crowd out the more profitable ones.

So how much should we sell our Apple Turnovers so that they are profitable?

That depends on many things. Competition is one factor to consider. If there is another bakery down the street that sells their Apple Turnovers for $1.50 each (the same as Mom's Bakery) then we really can't raise prices, or we might lose customers. In this case, we will have to rely on the Apple Turnovers to bring the clients in and then make our profit on other products (like coffee).

If on the other hand, there is no other bakery or competitor for miles around and Mom's Apple Turnovers are so good that people will drive for miles to buy them, then we can raise our prices quite a bit.

How much can we raise them?

That depends on something called, "Markup". You now know the cost to make them. Now you just need to know how much to sell them for.

And that actually is up to you. The secret here is that once you set a price it is very difficult to raise it. Increasing the prices of products is a very tricky thing to do because people will begin to reject your product. Even if you have loyal customers they will try to find a less expensive alternative. And when you start to lose customers you will also start to lose revenue and profits.

Unless, yes, there are always exceptions – unless you have a product that is what economists call, "Demand Inelastic". Which basically means that it does not matter the price because customers will still want it.

The high-end fashion industry is Demand Inelastic. (Have you seen the prices for Prada handbags or Jimmy Choo shoes? Oh yeah! Cheap they are not!)

But the problem then, is that you will have other companies creating cheap imitations of these goods and selling their cheap imitations for a lot less than the designers in the high-end fashion industry sell their real goods for. These cheap imitators are stealing sales. (No point crying about it. That is just how capitalism works.)

But Apple Turnovers are not Demand Inelastic. Therefore, we need to set a price for them that will be stable for the foreseeable future. That requires a good deal of research. Once again, we need to see what our competition is doing. Not just other bakeries but also supermarkets and even online gourmet Apple Turnover delivery services.

We need to:

List out the advantages of our product vs. competition

List what makes our company unique.

Here are some examples of our advantages:

1. Mom's Bakery Apple Turnovers are 100% natural made from all natural ingredients. As such they may qualify as kosher (if we can get a rabbi to approve them). Is there a Jewish community close by?

2. The Apple Turnovers are made fresh and served hot.

3. Mom's Bakery has a unique recipe that is a family secret (think Kentucky Fried Chicken).

4. As a result, you cannot get them anywhere else in the world.

Here are some examples of what makes our company unique:

1. We are family owned and not part of a huge faceless corporate conglomerate.

2. Our staff is friendly and always ready to give you a smile. (This is important for people like me who are morning grouches until we have had our second cup of coffee.)

3. We are the only bakery which is right next to the onramp for the freeway. All the morning traffic to downtown comes our way.

All of the above is stuff that I have made up as I go along. It will be different for your company. Just make sure that you list as many of these as you can. Then discuss them with other managers to get their feedback.

But now let us say that you have done all of the above and that you have decided that your markup should be 50%. That is to say, that you want to make a 50% profit on top of all of your costs. You know what your total costs are from what we did previously and that was $1.83 per Apple Turnover. How do you calculate the SELLING PRICE with a 50% markup? That is easy. Just multiply the cost of $1.83 by the inverse of the markup which is 1.5%. That gives us a selling price of $2.75 as follows.

Cost 1.83 x 1.5 = 2.75

Let's test this.

COST TO PRODUCE EACH APPLE TURNOVER		
Cost of Material:	$	0.49
Cost of Labor:	$	0.40
Cost of Overhead:	$	0.42
Total Costs to Produce	$	1.31
Total Cost to Sell Each Apple Trunover	$	0.52
Total Cost (Making and Selling):	$	1.83
Sales Price per Turnover		$2.75
Profit Margin per Turnover		$0.92

Now our profit margin per Apple Turnover is a positive .92 where as before, when we were selling them for $1.50 it was a loss of -.33 cents per Apple Turnover.

Then, if we divide the .92 cent profit by the cost of $1.83 we get a percent of 50%. That is our 50% markup.

So, our selling price is going to be $2.75 per Turnover. You may want to adjust this yearly (if you can) for the cost-of-living consumer price increase, (the CPI. Found on the Department of Commerce website.)

With a 50% markup you will have plenty of room to maneuver if you need to drop your prices in order to maybe clear out some extra inventory or bring in sales to other products.

Previously, I mentioned, when we saw that our Apple Turnovers were actually losing -.33 a turnover at a selling price of $1.50, that this sort of thing happens a lot.

Why is this?

The exercise that we just finished doing can be called Cost Accounting. Which is very different from Financial Accounting. In Financial Accounting the rules for valuing inventory are very simple. We use the cost of the material, then add the cost of the labor and finally also add in the cost of the manufacturing overhead.

One problem with this is that other costs are not included (such as selling costs) as we have just seen. Therefore, what Cost Accounting is really concerned with is putting reports and information in the hands of managers that they can use to determine the cost and profit relationship of their products. Financial Accounting is concerned with creating reports for managers AND outside parties such as investors or bankers. These reports need to follow a set criteria of rules called GAAP (acronym for Generally Accepted Accounting Principles).

But these rules just serve to tell us if the company is profitable or not. What we have just done (and what Cost Accounting does) is try to tell us if each and every product is profitable or not.

And this is a very important thing. Although I have been a consultant to companies where the president of the company felt that their company was profitable, and they don't need more complication in their lives. (Thank you very much for stopping by Mr. Planz and please don't let the door smack you in the butt on the way out.)

Then, what will inevitably happen is that one day, profit margins will start to slide, and they have no idea why.

This type of analysis will tell them why.

Also, if you are not pricing your products correctly then you are giving up profit for complacence. Not a good thing to do in a competitive business environment.

This type of analysis will give them important information on how to manage their profitability and then address problems when they come up.

Without this type of exercise – and information – managers will try to cut costs in order to boost falling profit margins. But these things are generally short-term solution that create long term problems.

For example, (to repeat myself – sorry), a company might see that profit margins are falling and then decide that they will cut the workforce by a certain percent. Maybe less customer service people. Or less quality control people. In the short run this will boost profit margins. But in the long run the company will suffer because their clients will be dissatisfied with their products or with the service. And they will take their business to another company that they feel values them more as customers.

But now that we have established what the real cost is of our Apple Turnovers let us plug the new price of $2.75 per turnover into our

Income Statement and see how that shakes out. Remember that we sell 100 turnovers a day. Given a 365-day year that means:

100 Turnovers a Day x 365 Days x $2.75 each = $100,375.

If we remember from our previous income statement, the breakdown of total sales for the year by product was $267,010 as follows:

- Apple Turnovers: about 100 sold a day at $1.50 each times 365 days a year is $54,750
- Coffee: About 200 cups a day at $2.00 each times 365 a year is $146,000.
- Custom Cakes: One a month for an average of about $200 each is $2,400.
- Other pastries: About 50 a day at $1.28 each times 365 days is $23,360.
- Juices: About 50 a day at $2.00 each times 365 days is $36,500
- Other incidental income is $4,000.
- <u>Grand Total Sales for the year is $267,010</u>

But if we now plug in $100,375 into the top row (substitute it for the $54,750) then our total sales for the year (including all of the other things we sell) is now $312,635 instead of $267,010. (Yes, there is that word – plug – again. Told you accountants love it.)

If we plug that into our income statement we get: (next page).

REVENUE	in $	In %
Gross Sales	$ 312,635	100%
Less Customer Discounts	$ (561)	0%
NET SALES	$ 312,074	100%
COST OF GOODS SOLD		
Beginning Inventory	$ 3,256	1%
Purchases	$ 76,000	24%
Less Ending Inventory	$ (2,358)	-1%
COST OF GOODS AVAILABLE for SALE	$ 76,898	25%
Production Direct Labor	$ 63,510	20%
Production Depreciation	$ 3,000	1%
Production Overhead	$ 3,000	1%
TOTAL COST of GOODS SOLD	$ 146,408	47%
GROSS PROFIT	$ 165,666	53%
SALES, GENERAL & OPERATING EXPENSES		
Advertising	$ 356	0%
Counter Sales Salaries & Wages	$ 65,850	21%
Rent	$ 18,000	6%
Supplies	$ 12,575	4%
Maintenance	$ 79	0%
Utilities	$ 596	0%
Depreciation - Store	$ 2,000	1%
Miscellaneous	$ 287	0%
TOTAL SALES, GENERAL & OPERATING EXPENSES	$ 99,743	32%
NET PROFIT	$ 65,923	21%

Our tentative net profit is $65,923. Much better than $20,298 isn't it?

Remember that this amount of net profit is "pure" for lack of a better word because all we did was increase the price. Everything else stayed the same. In other words. We did not make any more Apple Turnovers. If we had – say if we increased the daily amount of 100 a day to 150 a day – then our costs would have gone up also. But since the only change was in the price then everything else stays the same.

NOTE: There are more scientific ways of pricing your product but that will involve higher mathematics. For a discussion of this (if you have the stomach for it), see Appendix A.

THE COST – BENEFIT ANALYSIS

There are several ways to determine if an investment is going to be worthwhile. Whatever that investment may be. It could be a particular stock or bond, a new piece of machinery for your factory, a new factory in China, whatever it is that you want to invest in you will want to do it because it will bring you more profit.

For us, that is the key word, PROFIT.

Investment analysis has many exotic terms such as Internal Rate of Return, Hurdle Rate, Net Present Value, etc.

All of these are useful within what they are designed to evaluate. The Internal Rate of Return (also known as IRR), for example, is a special sort of interest rate that is set by the investor. It is what he wants to have if he (or she) is going to invest in that asset. The Hurdle rate is basically the same thing except for investments that are considered risky. The Net Present value (also known as NPV) is a way to determine what the future value of an investment is going to be TODAY if we hold that investment for a certain period of time. We usually take alternate investments and compare them to see which has the highest NPV. If we really want to get funky we do it with after tax dollars. [1]

---

[1] The idea behind NPV is to project all of the future cash inflows and outflows associated with an investment, discount all those future cash flows to the present day, and then add them together. The mathematical formula is:

$$NPV = \frac{R_t}{(1+i)^t}$$

That really makes it fun. (Told you I am a nurd.)

But we don't have to do any of that.

We just need to compare the cost, versus the benefit of a potential asset that we want to buy. Just to see if it really will have any benefits for us.

There are certain costs that we **do not** want to do this sort of analysis for. These are known as sunk costs. And these are costs that we have to make in order to be in business. An example of this would be the deposit that Mom made for the rental on the retail space for Mom's Bakery. Another example would be the decorations and leasehold improvements that she made to the shop in order to get it ready to receive customers, (cash registers, counters, coffee makers, etc.)

What we need to analyze are costs that we DON'T have to make. But which might just benefit us in the long run.

So, for example, let us say that Mom is thinking of buying an industrial mixer for the bakery. The mixer is a large piece of equipment that will mix large amounts of dough automatically.

The problem is this; at the bakery, the bakers are mixing the dough by hand. This limits the amount of dough that they mix to small batches. This in turn means repetitive mixing throughout the day. It is a time-consuming chore that forces production to run in small batches. In a manufacturing operation that is inefficient. Ideally all manufacturing companies want long production runs because that lowers the cost per unit. (Except Ferrari – that is why a New Ferrari costs about $700,000). The immediate cost is that the bakers have to work overtime in order to get ready for the next day's sales.[2]

Let us say that they average about ten hours of overtime in total per week. That is 40 hours per month. At $7.50 an hour that then becomes $15 an hour in overtime pay per hour. That is $150 a week or about $600 a month. Or, $7,200 a year.

The new industrial mixer will cost $3,000. If we buy the mixer then there would not be overtime (a simplification but good enough for this example).

Very simply, and by dividing $3,000 by $600 we can see that the mixer will pay for itself in five months.

$$\$3,000 / \$600 \text{ a month} = 5 \text{ months}$$

This sort of analysis is called the Payback Period. In other words, how much time needs to pass before the investment pays us back in savings. It is fundamental for all capital investments. Once upon a time I was the financial controller for a division of Westinghouse. The corporate rules were that any capital investment had to have a Payback Period of a maximum of three years. That is after tax. That was their rule. Every company is different.

---

[2] A Long Production Run is a manufacturing process where the maximum number of units are produced once the manufacturing process is set up.

If we continue our analysis of the mixer for Mom's Bakery we can also see that if the Payback Period is five months then that gives us a potential benefit of $600 a month for the remaining seven months of the year.

$$\$600 \times 7 \text{ months} = \$4{,}200$$

Which means that not only will the machine pay for itself in five months, but it will also give us a benefit of $4,200 in that first year. And a benefit of $7,200 for every year after that.

Looks like a good investment to me.

THE FINANCIAL LIFE CYCLE OF YOUR BUSINESS
FINANCING YOUR BUSINESS

There are three stages to the financial life cycle of your business:

1. THE SEED STAGE.
2. THE OUTSIDE FINANCING STAGE.
3. THE VENTURE CAPITAL OR GOING PUBLIC STAGE.

We will now discuss all three in sequence.

THE SEED STAGE

This is the most critical stage. Most new companies never make it out of this stage. The financial information firm, Dun & Bradstreet once did a study and found out that about 80% of all new companies fail within the first three years of existence.

When we were speaking about how Mom's Bakery got its start we left a question unanswered. And that was: how does she finance her growth? We can see that sales only provides a small percentage of what she needs to grow. Maybe somewhere between 10% to 30%. The rest – well the rest she will have to – scrounge for. (Sorry, couldn't think of a better term).

Basically, she will have to take out a second (or third) mortgage on her house. Use credit cards, personal loans, savings, and any other means that is legal. (We will not discuss what is illegal – sorry.)

In fact, finding capital is one of the most important things that a new business can do. But there are other things that are also important:

- Maintaining product quality.
- Expanding market share.
- Finding good employees.
- Controlling costs.
- Making good short term business decisions.
- Making good long-term business decisions.
- Maintaining positive cash flow.

It is, in effect, a wonderful balancing act.

Of all the things that you must concentrate on from that nice long list above, the most important (they are all important), but if I had to choose as to which one is critical to the survival of any business – that would be cash flow.

You will have trouble finding financing. There is no bank that will lend money to a business that is less than three years old. They will lend against any equity you may have as personal equity. That means your home, your car, cash deposits, etc. SBA loans are good, but they will want to take anything not nailed down (as well as everything that is nailed down – as collateral). The advantage of an SBA loan is that the government will guarantee the loan to the bank. If the loan goes bad the government will pay the bank 90 cents on the dollar.

But, probably, the biggest source of financing for your new business is going to be leaning on your vendors. In fact, and you will probably be surprised when you hear this, but the largest source of business financing in the United States is not from banks, venture capital or the stock market. It is in fact the trade credit (a company's vendors).

Most companies when they sell on credit (also referred to as "Terms"), will give you 30 days to pay them. Others will give you terms called, "2/10 net 30". That means if you pay the invoice in 10 days then you can take 2% off from the full amount of the invoice. So, for example, if a vendor sends you an invoice for $1,000 with the terms, 2/10 net 30, and you pay that invoice within 10 days then you can take 2% off from the total amount of the invoice ($1,000 x 2% = $20). That means that you will only have to send the vendor $980.

It may not seem like a lot, but if you think about it, a $20 discount every 30 days adds up to about $243 a year. At most companies. The invoices are for far more than $1,000. If the invoice is for $10,000 then your savings for that year will be $2,433. If the interest is 2% every 30 days then that is an effective rate of interest of about 24% in your favor (2% every 30 days is 2% 12 times a year = 24%).

The other side of that coin is that your clients will also play the same game with you. You want to get paid as quickly as possible so that you can cover your production expenses. But your clients will want to hold off payment as long as possible.

Why not? Heck! It's an interest free loan.

That is why when I was a financial manager I did away with the 2/10 net 30 concept and started to charge our clients interest at the rate of 15% a year.

My terms were then, Net 30. We will charge you interest at the rate of 15% a year after 30 days. And by the way; that means compounded interest.

Naturally, there was a lot of weeping and wailing as well as hand wringing from our clients. But I had the advantage in that my bargaining power was stronger. They needed our products. And our products had better quality than our competitors. Yes, there is that word once again – quality.

The other thing that you can do is to simply cut the client off if the debt becomes too large. I had clients that would buy from us on a weekly basis in the amounts of between $30,000 to $50,000 dollars. They would hold off payment for up to 60 days. That would bring their balance up to about $200,000. At that point I would cut them off until they brought all of their invoices current. (Yes, more weeping and wailing – but they paid. Then the game would start all over again.)

All of these are things that you will have to determine for yourself. Every industry is different, and every company is also different.

Is there a written contract to all of this? Yes and no. (Spoken like a lawyer right?)

There is no formal written contract such as in a car loan or a mortgage. What there is, is a series of documents which form a contract. For example, you want to buy something from a vendor and send him a Purchase Order (PO for short). He then sends you the merchandise and an invoice. All of those are part of the contract according to the Uniform Commercial Code. In addition to this there are letters, emails, memos, etc. All of that goes into account of the formation of that contract. Yes, a whole bunch of paperwork. It might surprise you to know that over 75% of all commercial transactions in the United Sates take are made under this criteria instead of a written contract.

THE OUTSIDE FINANCING STAGE

Once you grow enough in terms of revenue (and cash flow) you will get to the next stage of the company growth called the Outside Financing Stage. If you have made it to this stage then you need to give yourself a big pat on the back.

Now you will qualify for a commercial bank loan. Basically, that is what this stage is all about.

You have survived the seed stage and have built up a company that is stable as well as profitable. Well, most of the time.

Banks love companies like yours. They will try to sell you loan products that they think you need.

Be wary.

Most bankers don't know how a small growing company works or what it needs. Stay away from asset-based lenders because they will strangle your company.

Stay away from lines of credit that need to be fully repaid every year.

Term loans are good. They are usually for five years.

SBA loans are for companies that do not qualify for normal bank financing. The SBA will go through a bank. The SBA will guarantee your loan. If the loan goes south the SBA will pay the loan back to the bank at .90 cents on the dollar.

For any kind of loan, the bank (and the SBA) will take as collateral everything in the business that they can.

This includes all of your inventory and accounts receivable.

Also, they will take your personal guarantee. That means that if the loan goes south they (the bank and the SBA) will come after your personal assets.

In California, business owners used to be partially protected by the one-step rule. That means that lenders can come after your personal assets once. They cannot go back to court and get a deficiency judgement.

Returning to the issue of asset-based lenders.

Why are they a bad idea? The asset-based lenders will control your accounts receivables. They will collect on them and then lend you a certain amount of money based on what they feel the value is.

The problem is that they are limiting the amount of cash that a growing company gets. And remember, the one thing that a growing company needs is cash. This is critical. But you will not be able to grow your company if the cash that you have available is limited.

What a growing company really needs is a Permanent Working Capital Line of Credit. A Permanent Working Capital Line of Credit is a combination of a line of credit and a term loan. You can borrow on the line of credit up to a certain amount. After that it becomes a term loan.

The important thing about this is that you (as the company) control your accounts receivables. That is one source of cash flow. Then the line of credit from the bank is the secondary source of cash flow.

NOTE:

If you want to learn more about how a Permanent Working Capital Line of Credit works, as well as about finance in general then you may want to read my book, "The Banker" which is on sale at amazon.com.

THE VENTURE CAPITAL or PUBLIC OFFERING STAGE

Now you have reached the final stage in the financial life cycle of your business.

Your business is now profitable and running smoothly – well – almost.

But you have big plans, and you want to expand. You need more capital than what the banks are willing to lend you.

You decide to approach, or alternatively, you are approached by a venture capital firm.

They will want to invest a certain sum in your business in exchange for a percent ownership in the business.

This has its pros and its cons. On one hand, these people are very financially sophisticated and that can help you.

On the other hand, they might take over the business. They will make key decisions including who you hire, fire, etc.

Nor will any of this be for free. They will charge you for their consulting time and for their travel expenses. Nor will any of this be cheap. Some of them make up to $5,000 a day. If one of the partners spends a day at your company you will have to pay that.

Also, it is not a carte blanche. They will contract with you to give you a certain amount. Say for example, $5,000,000. There may be escalation clauses where they will give you more if you meet certain criteria. But also, there will most likely be a "Burn Rate".

If your company is building market share but losing money, the burn rate is the rate at which you are going through the money they give you. That is the definition of Burn Rate put in simple terms. It can be in many forms. But generally, if your company is losing $1,000,000 a year and you were given $5,000,000 then your burn rate is five years. If you exceed your burn rate the venture capital firm will walk away, and you will be on your own again. Which means that they expect you to become profitable.

Now remember, your company may be making a good net profit but have negative cash flow (this is normal for young growing companies). Or it may be experiencing bad net profit results but have good cash flow (this is normal for companies that are on the downward cycle of their existence.)

What you need to remember are two things:

All of these things are negotiable.

Also, The Venture Capital Stage is not necessarily the final stage of your company's financial growth. It may come at the beginning.

Your product may be so unique, and you may also have a patent for this product which is very valuable. In which case the Venture Capital Stage may be an option for you from the start.

Of course, what the venture capital firms ultimately want is to take your company public. That is how they make their money.

Generally, they use their own money, as well as that of their investors, to find young companies with great potential. Their job is to nurse those companies to appoint where they can go public (be traded on a stock exchange).

There are three types of Venture Capital Investment:

1. Pre-Seed: The founders of a company try to turn an idea (or a product) into a real business (not just an idea). They may have a patent on a product or idea that some investors feel will be valuable. The venture capitalists will ensure funding and guidance.
2. Seed Funding: Here the existing business will try to launch a new product. The difference with pre-seed funding is that at this stage the founders of the company have already invested some of their money.
3. Early-Stage Funding: This is where a business is established and is already selling a product (or various products) and needs more capital to expand its growth.

This is the end of this discussion.

Now comes the last part of this discussion and that is – going public. Which means that you will sell shares of your company to the public on a recognized stock exchange. Most likely this will be NASDAQ (National Association of Securities Dealers Automated Quotations)

This is the promised land of most entrepreneurs. The Nirvana of Capitalism. This is where all of your hard work pays off. When you take your company public you will become one of the wealthy elite. Maybe millions of dollars. Maybe billions.

The path here is not easy. What is important for you to remember are three things:

1. In order to go public, you will need at least three years of audited financial statements. I can tell you from experience that this will be tremendously expensive. Why? Because most young companies do not have clean financial statements. Nor even an organized financial process or department. I have made a small fortune charging $150 to $235 an hour to go back and reorganize, re-examine, re-analyze and then restate those three years of financial statements. Doing that sort of forensic accounting is a very specialized field. Therefore, my advice is to make sure that all of your ducks are lined up as far as financial reporting is concerned so that you will not need to hire someone like me. I have told this to businesspeople over and over again. And fortunately (for me) none of them have paid attention. Huh! Go figure.

2. When you do go public the investment bankers will give you two options for offering the shares of your company. One is the best-efforts basis and the other is the fixed price basis. If they use the best-efforts basis then they will try to float your shares and try to get the best price possible. What the open market will price the shares at. If they use the fixed price basis they will offer your shares at a certain price. If the market starts to slip then they will use their own money

(going into the market to buy your shares on their account) to boost the price.

3. Going public means that your independence is over. You will have a board of directors telling you how to do things and evaluating you. Also, you will have the Securities and Exchange Commission looking over your shoulder. (The SEC).

And that is all there is. (Just like the old Peggy Lee song). What I have tried to do is to give you a very basic understanding of finance and how to make a business grow and succeed.

I have spoken of other things such as cash flow and going public.

These are other things for a more detailed discussion. I will be conducting those other discussion in the future. If you feel that you have enough knowledge now for what is at hand then good. I am glad to have helped.

If you would like to learn more then I will give future discussions on cash flow, forecasting and budgeting.

Hope to see you there.

And – last item: Remember in the beginning when I said that it is important to remember that in life you get what you pay for?

I am specifically speaking of getting good accounting help. I have worked with many companies that have put the accounting department on the back burner. They have concentrated on sales, marketing, product development, etc.

But a good accountant is a very important piece of the puzzle. Because in the end – business is all about money. And accounting is the language of business. There are a lot of charlatans out there – even CPA's who say that they understand a growing business. That is most likely false. I have spent a considerable part of my career fixing problems that other accountants (CPAs included) have created.

Many people get into the profession because it seems easy. Only adding or subtracting, debits, credits, etc. But in order to do this well you have to both, be able to think abstractly AND be able to have an organized mind. That is a rare talent.

But a good accountant can help you succeed. And a really good accountant can make you very wealthy.

Also, when I was in college, I learned that there are three types of people in this world.

1. The generalists: These people only see the big picture. They do not get into the details of anything. And if they do they usually get frustrated and quit.

2. The details people: They love to get into the weeds and ruminate over the details of everything they touch. They do not see the big picture. If you try to talk the big picture to them they will just give you a blank stare.

3. The folks who are both of the above: These guys can deal with the details and then change gears and see the big picture also.

There are many folks who are either Generalists or Detail people. The folks who can do both – well – there are not many of those. Yet these are the guys who you want to be in charge of your accounting department. They are hard to find. And they are expensive.

I have also seen companies that have invested in the lowest priced accounting professional as well as accounting software. In time they will call me in (or someone like me) to fix the mess. This can be EXTREMELY expensive. People like me do not come cheap. And it is often more expensive to fix the mess than if you did things right from the start.

I have two examples: One is a gentleman who was an engineer and decided to start a company that made airplane parts. He used a part-time bookkeeper and QuickBooks. None of his accounting records were in order. When it came time to sell the company (he wanted to retire) he sold it for a price of about $2M to a large aerospace company where he could have sold it for at least ten times that amount. Perhaps more. Mostly, companies are valued at about ten times yearly cash flow. Depending on the company and depending on the industry. But no one could determine what the cash flow of this company was because he did not have good financial records. I was working at ITT at the time and that is the company that bought this other company. After reorganizing his accounting books, I saw that he could have sold it for about $23M. yes, the gentleman left $21M on the table.

Another example is a small company that wanted to go public in order to get more cash and to continue growing. But in order to go public you need at least three years of audited financial statements. Because their financial statements were not in order there was no CPA firm that would touch it. And consequently – no investment banker would go near it. This company will probably not survive.

Now, I have come across people in my career that have been dismissive of a professional's curriculum vitae by saying, "Too much experience!," or "Overqualified!"

But if you are in a young growing company what are you going to do? Find a person with just the right amount of experience for the job now?

Then, as the company grows and becomes more complicated, find someone else with just that amount of experience? Then as it grows some more – get rid of those people with "just the right amount of experience" and then hire someone else with a higher level of qualifications but again, "just the right amount of experience?"

I will argue that it would be better to find someone who is overqualified from the start so that that person can guide you successfully through the growth process.

But very qualified people are expensive. Again, it is a balancing act. There are no easy answers.

Also, in my professional career I have come across employers who are looking for someone with "Ten years" experience doing something for one company. (Like corporate controller, financial analyst, etc.)

But how long does it take to learn anything? Certainly not ten years. If you hire someone like that you will have a person who has ten years of experience doing the same thing over and over again. So, basically – one year of experience at doing the same thing over and over. Or, one year of experience multiplied by ten. What good is that?

One of my favorite professors in college once told me, "Find someone who has different experiences doing different things in different industries. Because that person will bring a lot more insight as well as new ideas into the job process than the person who has been doing the same thing over and over again for ten years."

In academic circles they refer to this as gaining curriculum. You get your bachelor's degree at one university then your master's at another and finally your Ph.D. at still another.

It is all about getting different points of view and of understanding different ways of doing something.

Then the question is, how do you find a good financial person? How can you tell the real deal from the charlatans?

Well….. you read books like this one.

APPENDIX A

I must warn you that if you are not a qualified member of the International Nurds Association then reading this section will completely freak you out.

Proceed with care!

(LOL)

Anyway.

Let us say that we have a company that sells a whatchamacallit, (widget for short), for $20 each. Let us also say that at the moment the company sells 50,000 of these widgets a year.

What is our revenue? Very simply, Total Revenue is Price x Quantity. Or:

Revenue = R

Price = P

Quantity = Q

R = P x Q

If we substitute the numbers into the equation we get

R = $20 per widget x 50,000 units sold

Or

R = $ 1,000,000

So, total revenue for our widgets is $1,000,000 a year. The question then comes up; how much can we raise the price of our widgets to maximize the revenue of the product? We want the revenue to be more than a mere $1,000,000 a year. The only way to do this is to increase the price. But then there is the problem that if we do increase the price we will lose some customers and that, would lower revenue. Which in effect, would defeat the purpose of raising prices to begin with.

What a conundrum right?

Well then, is there a price that we can increase the sale of each widget by that will increase revenue anyway even if some of our customers do in fact go away?

Yes, there is. How do we find that?

Let us say that we have a real whiz bang marketing department. And after much polling of the customers and lots of number crunching they determine that if we increase the price by $3 (sell them for $23 instead of $20) we will lose 3,000 customers.

Some executives will say, we only lose 3,000 customers out of 50,000 customers? That is no big deal lets raise the price anyway.

But!

Yes, but!

We still need to know what the total revenue will be if we increase the price to $23 and then lose 3,000 customers.

Therefore, we now have two prices "P" and two quantities "Q".

The first price is $20 (the original price), and we will call that P1. The second price is $23, and we will call that P2.

Our first quantity is 50,000 customers and we will call that Q1. Our second quantity is 50,000 customers – 3,000 customers and that gives us 47,000 customers. We will call 47,000 customers Q2.

A change between two numbers can be described as the slope of a line. If we put that into a mathematical equation we can describe it as:

$$\frac{Q2 - Q1}{P2 - P1}$$

Let substitute our Ps' and Qs' with numbers:

$$\frac{47,000 - 50,000}{23 - 20}$$ (This describes change over change or M over M)

Which becomes

$$\frac{-3,000}{3}$$

This becomes -1,000. Let us call this M.

In order to get to where we where we want to go we will need to use a little bit of higher algebra.

We will use the equation for the slope of a line which is:

$$Y = MX + B$$

Where Y = Q (or quantity)

$\quad$ M = -1,000

$\quad$ X = P (or price)

Then, all we need to do is find the Y intercept which is B. Let's put some numbers in the equation:

50,000 = -1,000($20) + B

Using simple algebra:

<u>Step 1</u>.
Multiply the -1,000 times the 20 = -20,000.

Our equation then becomes:

50,000 = -20,000 + B

Step 2.
We move the -20,000 to the left side of the equation by adding both sides of the "=" by positive 20,000

20,000 + 50,000 = -20,000 + B + 20,000

On the right side of the equation the positive and negative 20,000 – 20,000 cancel out and leave us with zero.
On the left side the 20,000 + the 50,000 added together give us 70,000.

In other words,

B = 70,000

Since B is the Y intercept this means that

Q = -1,000P + 70,000

If we go back to our original Revenue equation of R = PQ

Then

R = P (-1,000P + 70,000)

 (this little symbol means "Therefore")

R = -1,000 P^2 + 70,000 P (The Quadratic Equation)

Almost done!

Now all we need to do is find the X point in the slope of the line by using the algebraic function for Height which is:

$$H \text{ (height)} = -\left（\frac{B}{2A}\right)$$

Where B = 70,000

A = -1,000

$$H = -\left(\frac{70{,}000}{2(-1{,}000)}\right)$$

And that gives us that H = $35.00

Or, our optimum price will not be $23 as we originally thought. It will actually be $35.

This can be shown graphically as a bell-shaped curve where the $35 is at the top of the bell.

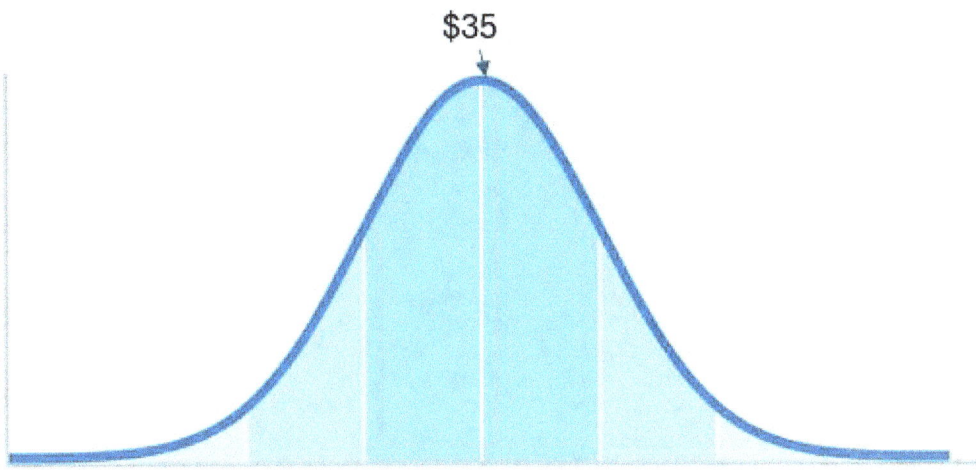

In order to calculate what the total revenue will be at our new price of $35 then we just need to go back to our Quadratic equation and put the numbers in:

R = -1,000 ($35)² + 70,000 ($35)

If we solve for Revenue (the "R"), we get

R = $1,225,000

Our optimum revenue then, at the new price of $35 will be $1,225,000 from $1,000,000.

When companies do this they do it continually to examine the outcome versus what they equation told them. It might be that they did not lose 3,000 customers as expected. Maybe they only lost 1,000 customers. In which case the total revenue would be higher.

But it is something that must be tested over and over again in order to get the best results.

www.ingramcontent.com/pod-product-compliance
Lightning Source LLC
Chambersburg PA
CBHW062221220526
45471CB00009B/3297